A NATION ONLINE:
HOW AMERICANS ARE EXPANDING THEIR USE OF THE INTERNET

A NATION ONLINE: HOW AMERICANS ARE EXPANDING THEIR USE OF THE INTERNET

ROGER E. CLANCY (ED.)

Novinka Books
New York

Senior Editors: Susan Boriotti and Donna Dennis
Coordinating Editor: Tatiana Shohov
Office Manager: Annette Hellinger
Graphics: Wanda Serrano
Editorial Production: Jennifer Vogt, Matthew Kozlowski and Maya Columbus
Circulation: Ave Maria Gonzalez, Indah Becker, Raymond Davis and Vladimir Klestov
Communications and Acquisitions: Serge P. Shohov
Marketing: Cathy DeGregory

Library of Congress Cataloging-in-Publication Data
Available Upon Request

ISBN: 1-59033-339-X

Copyright © 2002 by Novinka Books, An Imprint of
        Nova Science Publishers, Inc.
        400 Oser Ave, Suite 1600
        Hauppauge, New York 11788-3619
        Tele. 631-231-7269   Fax 631-231-8175
        e-mail: Novascience@earthlink.net
        Web Site: http://www.novapublishers.com

Printed in the United States of America

CONTENTS

Preface — vii

Chapter 1   **Overview** — 1

Chapter 2   **Computer and Internet Use** — 9

Demographic Factors in Computer and Internet Use — 11

Chapter 3   **Online Activities** — 35

Primary Uses by the U.S. Population — 35
Activities among Those Individuals Online — 36

Chapter 4   **How and Where America Goes Online** — 43

Connection Types: The Expansion of Broadband — 43
Spread of New Devices — 46
Location of Use — 47

Chapter 5   **The Digital Generation: How Young People have Embraced Computers and the Internet** — 53

Computer and Internet Use — 53
The Impact of Schools on Internet and Computer Use — 56
How Young People are Using the Internet — 65
Concerns about Children's Online Use — 66

Chapter 6   **The Digital Workplace** — 71

Introduction — 71
Computer Use at Work by Occupation — 72
Computer Use at Work by Gender and Age — 73

Types of Computer Uses at Work   74
Internet Use at Work   76
The Work – Home Connection   78

**Chapter 7   Computer and Internet Use among
                 People with Disabilities**   **81**

People with Disabilities   81

Chapter 8   The Unconnected   **91**

The Offline Population   91
The Importance of Cost to Households Never Connected to the Internet   93
Why Households have Discontinued Internet Access   95
Effect of Confidentiality Concerns   96
Content Concerns   96
The Role of Network Effects   97

**Chapter 9   Reductions in Inequality for
                 Computer and Internet Use**   **111**

Conclusion   116
Methodology   117

Index   **119**

PREFACE

This book provides comprehensive information on Americans' connectivity to the Internet, broadband services, and computers. Increasing numbers of Americans have integrated these technologies into their daily lives and are using them in a variety of places and for a wide range of activities.

The expanding use of new technologies continues to strengthen the economy. More Americans an now engage in online commerce, obtain e-government services, and access valuable information. Broadband connections are also on the rise. These high-speed connections will make it easier for people to engage in distance learning programs or telemedicine and to access a whole new array of entertainment and services that are on the horizon.

Chapter 1

OVERVIEW

Americans' use of information technologies grew at phenomenal rates in 2001. This past year saw a rapid increase in computer and Internet use, not only in homes, but also at the workplace, schools, and other locations. Broadband connections, available principally through cable modems and digital subscriber lines (DSL), are making higher-speed connections available to an increasing number of Americans and expanding options for online usage.

The Department of Commerce's Census Bureau surveyed approximately 57,000 households containing more than 137,000 individuals in all fifty states and the District of Columbia and found a rapid diffusion of these technologies.[1] At the time of the survey, September 2001, 60.2 million U.S. homes (or 56.5 percent) had a personal computer. Seven of every eight households with computers (88.1 percent) also subscribed to the Internet. As a result, more than half of U.S. households (53.9 million homes, or 50.5 percent) had Internet connections. As shown in Figure 1-1, this remarkable rise to over 50 percent household penetration of both computers and the Internet occurred very quickly.[2]

On an individuals (rather than household) basis, as of September 2001 as of September 2001, 143 million people in the United States (or 53.9 percent) were using the Internet, up from 116.5 million people (or 44.5 percent) in August 2000. Two-thirds (66.8 percent) of the people in the United States used a computer at home, school and/or work. The vast majority of those who used computers (80.6 percent) were also connecting to the Internet. These two factors taken together contributed to a

---

[1] For a more extensive discussion on the U.S. Census Bureau's survey methods in the Current Population Survey Supplement, see the Methodology section at the end of this report.

[2] Households with at least one computer plus Internet connectivity total 53.0 million. A number of households also have more than one Internet access device. See Chapter 4 for a more detailed discussion.

substantial rise in Internet use. By September 2001, .143 million people in the United States (or 53.9 percent) were using the Internet, up from 116.5 million people (or 44.5 percent) in August 2000. The widespread increase in information technologies in the United States has occurred across all 50 states. As Figure 1-2 shows, in August 2000, few states had more than 50 percent of their population using the Internet. By September 2001, most states had at least half of their population online. Table 1-1 provides a state-by-state breakdown of individual Internet use.

Figure 1-1: Percent of U.S. Households with a Computer and Internet Connections, Selected Years

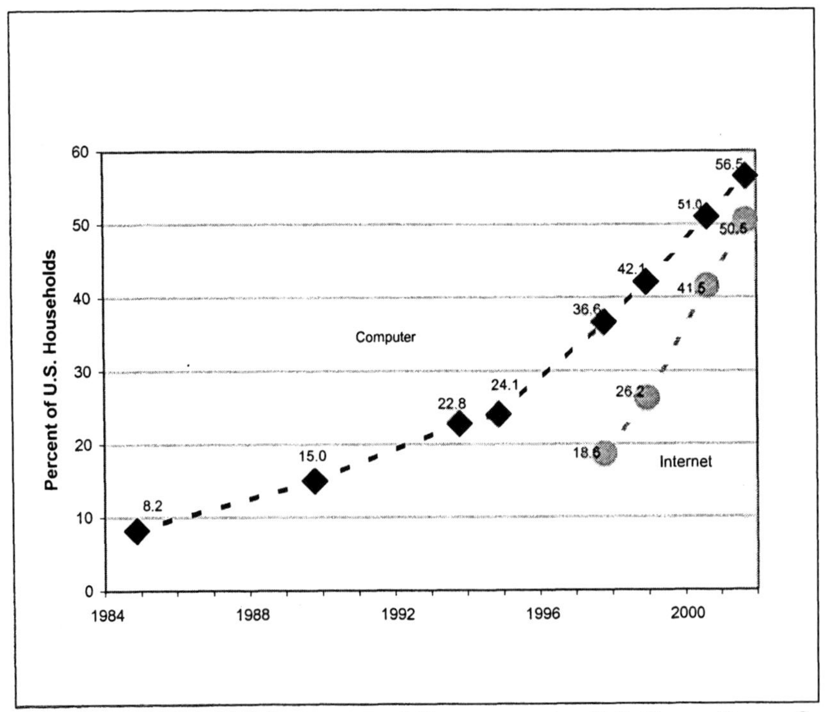

Source: NTIA and ESA, U.S. Department of Commerce, using U.S. Census Bureau Current Population Survey Supplements.

Figure 1-2: The Rapid Increase in Internet Use in the United States Across States

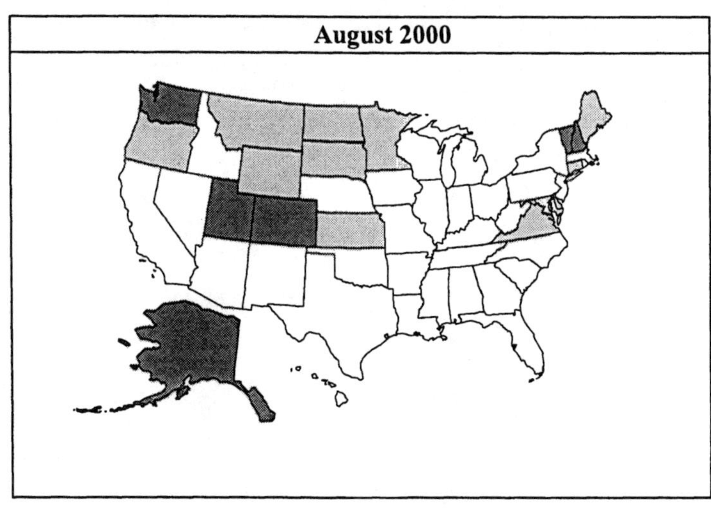

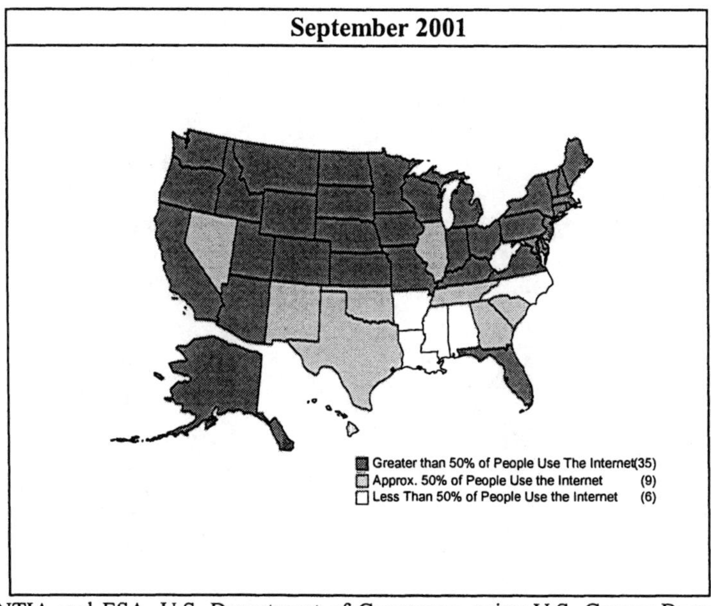

Source: NTIA and ESA, U.S. Department of Commerce, using U.S. Census Bureau Current Population Survey Supplements.

Table 1-1. Internet Use by Percent of State Population

State	Total Population, Age 3+ Thousands)	Percent Who Are Internet Users (90 Percent Confidence Interval)*
Alabama	4,271	43.3 — 49.0
Alaska	593	66.0 — 71.6
Arizona	4,641	50.4 — 55.8
Arkansas	2,544	41.4 — 47.1
California	33,108	50.9 — 53.3
Colorado	4,004	57.3 — 62.9
Connecticut	3,170	55.3 — 61.9
DC	509	42.0 — 48.6
Delaware	732	55.1 — 61.6
Florida	15,075	50.5 — 53.5
Georgia	7,550	47.7 — 52.8
Hawaii	1,150	47.6 — 54.1
Idaho	1,244	53.0 — 58.5
Illinois	11,486	49.5 — 53.0
Indiana	5,733	52.6 — 58.4
Iowa	2,769	55.3 — 61.2
Kansas	2,509	55.0 — 61.0
Kentucky	3,785	50.3 — 56.1
Louisiana	4,141	40.6 — 46.2
Maine	1,233	57.2 — 63.6
Maryland	5,115	58.4 — 64.3
Massachusetts	5,993	54.5 — 58.8
Michigan	9,553	54.6 — 58.2
Minnesota	4,742	60.7 — 66.2
Mississippi	2,642	38.9 — 44.7
Missouri	5,192	54.3 —60.3
Montana	866	54.7 — 60.4
Nebraska	1,632	52.4 — 58.4
Nevada	1,902	49.2 —54.9
New Hampshire	1,194	60.2 — 66.7
New Jersey	7,944	58.1 — 61.8
New Mexico	1,754	46.9 — 52.6
New York	17,510	51.6 — 54.3
North Carolina	7,200	45.0 — 49.3
North Dakota	591	53.4 — 59.5

State	Total Population, Age 3+ (Thousands)	Percent Who Are Internet Users (90 Percent Confidence Interval)*
Ohio	10,877	53.2 — 56.8
Oklahoma	3,161	46.8 — 52.5
Oregon	3,358	58.2 — 64.1
Pennsylvania	11,356	53.3 — 56.7
Rhode Island	943	53.3 — 60.0
South Carolina	3,728	44.6 — 50.7
South Dakota	690	55.9 — 61.6
Tennessee	5,209	49.5 — 55.5
Texas	19,576	49.7 — 52.6
Utah	2,061	58.7 — 64.0
Vermont	590	57.3 — 63.6
Virginia	6,653	55.7 — 61.2
Washington	5,661	58.3 — 64.2
West Virginia	1,712	43.9 — 49.5
Wisconsin	5,070	54.1 — 59.9
Wyoming	460	59.3 — 65.2

* Specific point estimates are subject to sampling error (see Methodology Section). This Table reports the 90 percent confidence interval to avoid inaccurate and misleading rankings of states by Internet use point estimates. With a probability of 90 percent the "true" percent of Internet use falls within this range.

The rapid diffusion of the Internet is not a unique U.S. phenomenon. According to data compiled by the Organization for Economic Cooperation and Development (OECD) from various nations, the rise in Internet use is truly a global phenomenon (Figure 1-3).[3]

---

[3] Other studies or reports that have identified this general trend among various countries include, but are not limited to, the Asian Pacific Economic Cooperation (APEC) Working Group on Telecommunications and Information (TEL), *Interim Response of the TEL to Leaders' Declaration Concerning Internet Issues*, 24th Meeting, Jejii Island, Korea, Doc. No. DCSG/2, September 29, 2001 (www.apectelwg.otg/apec/atwg); Conference Board of Canada, *Canada in 2nd Place on Connectedness Index*, February 13, 2001 (www.conferenceboard.ca/press/2001/connectedness); International Telecommunication Union (ITU), *World Telecommunication Development Report 2001*, Geneva, ITU, 2001; OECD, *The Digital Divide: Diffusion and Use of ICTS*, DSTI/ICCP/IE (2000)/Final, January 2002.

**Figure 1-3: Individuals Using the Internet from any
Location, Selected Countries, 1999 and 2000**

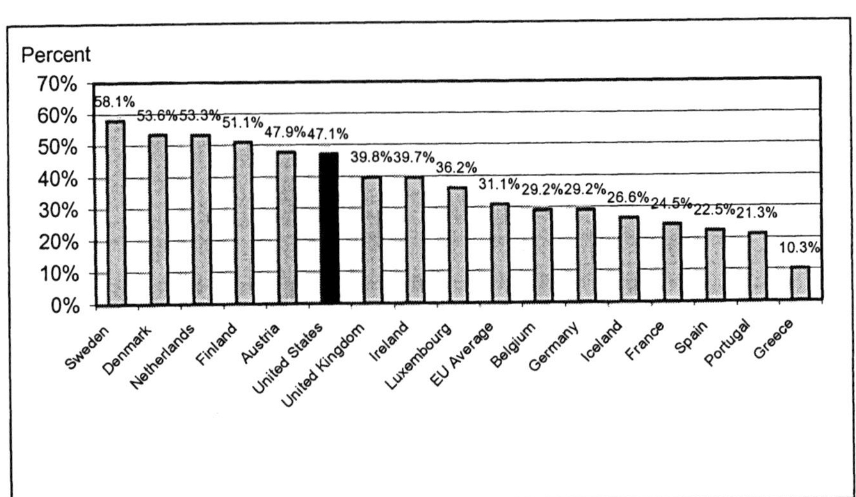

Note: EU country estimates are for February 2001 and US estimates are for August 2000.
Source: European Union, http://europa.eu.int/information_society/eeurope/index_en.htm and
U.S. Department of Commerce, Economic and Statistics Administration.

The spread of new technologies, such as the Internet, can be described by a variety of metrics – such as the percent of households connected (Figure 1-1) and the percent of the population connected (Figure 1-2). Figure 1-4 shows how selecting a different basis of measurement can affect the results: in September 2001, 50.5 percent of households had Internet connections; 56.7 percent of the total U.S. population lived in households with these connections; a lower 43.6 percent of Americans were using the Internet in their homes; while 53.9 percent of the total population used the Internet at some location.

This report features data on *individuals* more than data on *households*,[4] for several reasons. First, focusing on individuals permits us to study such factors as age, gender, education, and employment status in determining computer and Internet use. Second, Internet access is more frequently occurring outside the home, at such locations as work, schools, and libraries. And finally, a small but growing number of Internet connections is increasingly occurring over personal devices, such as wireless phones and personal digital assistants, in addition to the computer. For some variables, such as the type of home Internet connection and reasons for non-subscribership, the

---

[4] For additional information on *household* connectivity, see www.esa.doc.gov or www.ntia.doc.gov. These charts may be useful for international comparisons when households are the unit of measurement.

household remains the unit of measurement because that is the level at which the question was most appropriately asked.

Figure 1-4: Different Perspectives on Internet Access and Use

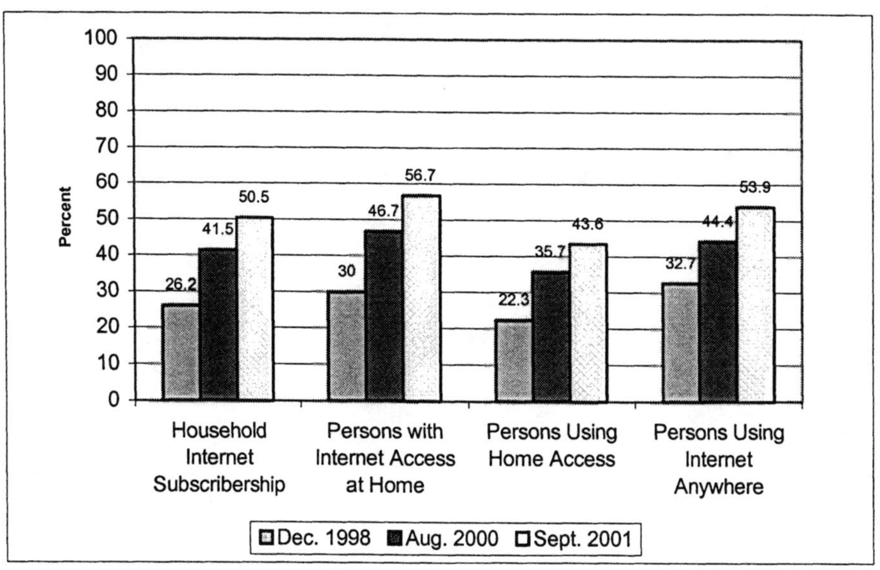

Source: NTIA and ESA, U.S. Department of Commerce, using U.S. Census Bureau Current Population Survey Supplements

This book examines computer and Internet use from a number of perspectives.

Chapter 2 provides an overview of the expanding use of computers and the Internet and how different demographics, such as income or age, are associated with rates of use.

Chapter 3 looks at online activities. It also examines the relationship of a variety of demographic factors to online activities.

Chapter 4 reports on how and where people are going online; the expanding use of broadband connections; and the small but growing number of people using secondary devices, such as mobile cell phones. Chapter 4 also examines a particularly significant development in the past year: the increasing use of the Internet outside the home.

Chapters 5 and 6 focus on particular "outside the home" locations: work and school. Chapter 5 examines how schools provide access to computers and the Internet for students, enabling children of all socio-economic backgrounds to use these technologies. As a result, children and young adults are among the highest users of new technologies, integrating the Internet in their schoolwork and other activities. Chapter 6 focuses on how use at the workplace has affected the presence and use of computers and the Internet at home.

Of course, not all Americans are using computers or the Internet at high rates. Chapter 7 examines how one such group—those with disabilities—still trails behind the national average in terms of use. Chapter 8 discusses more generally the population that is not online and considers some possible reasons for their lack of connectivity.

Finally, Chapter 9 examines changes in Internet and computer use for subgroups of the population over time. Using a standard methodology to gauge inequality, our research shows that inequality among various groups is decreasing. These trends continue, we expect that new information technologies will become more widely shared by an ever-expanding number of Americans.

Chapter 2

COMPUTER AND INTERNET USE

Increasingly, we are a nation online. Individuals continue to expand their use of computers and the Internet. As of September 2001, 174 million people or 65.6 percent of the U.S. population were computer users. One hundred forty three million people or 53.9 percent of the population used the Internet (Tables 2-1 and 2-2 and Figure 2-1).

Figure 2-1: Internet Use From Any Location, Percent of Persons Age 3 +

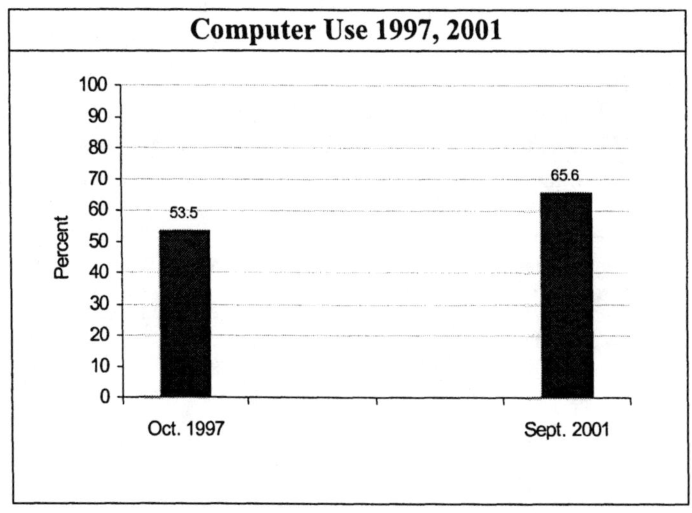

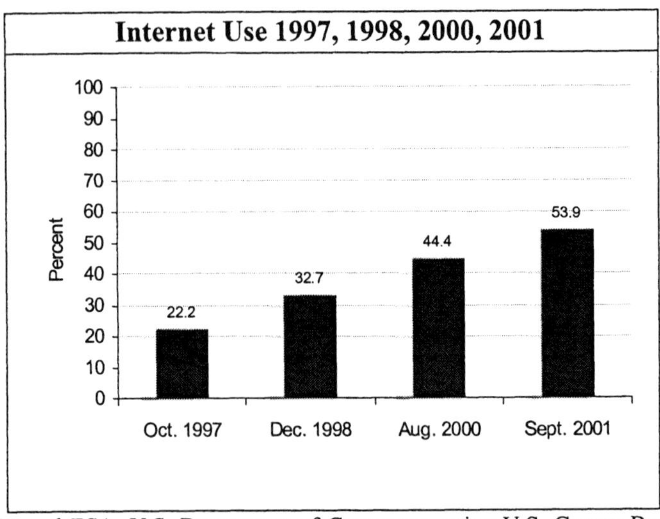

Source: NTIA and ESA, U.S. Department of Commerce, using U.S. Census Bureau Current Population Survey Supplements

Both computer and Internet use have increased substantially in the past few years. Since 1997 computer use has grown at a rate of 5.3 percent on an annualized basis.[5] Internet use has grown at a rate of 20 percent a year since 1998. In the thirteen months before September 2001, over 26 million more people went online.

The demographic profile of computer and Internet users provided in this chapter reveals that growth in computer and Internet use is broadly based. In every income bracket, at every level of education, in every age group, for people of every race and among people of Hispanic origin, among both men and women, many more people use computers and the Internet now than did so in the recent past. Some people are still

---

[5] Although the Current Population Survey Supplements (on which this report and reports in the *Falling Through the Net series* are based) have tracked computer penetration rates in the United States, they have done so on a *household* basis; *i.e.*, respondents have been asked to report whether there was a computer in the household. The 2001 survey, however, included questions on whether a person uses a computer. Because questions on individual computer use have not been asked since the October 1997 Current Population Survey Supplement, data on *computer use by individuals* are not available for 1998 and 2000.

The 1997 survey also used somewhat different phrasing for both the computer and Internet use questions. In 1997, respondents were asked about their use of "Internet and other online services" and their use of "personal or home computers, laptops, mini computers or mainframe computers." In 2001, respondents were asked about their use of the "Internet" and about their use of "personal computers and laptops." The computer use questions are roughly similar, although the 2001 data would likely be somewhat higher if respondents had been specifically instructed to include the use of "mini computers or mainframe computers" in their response. The Internet use question likely provides a correct order of magnitude for Internet use. The difference in the question's phrasing, however, makes the *comparison* of growth rates between 1997 and other years somewhat problematic. All growth rates are calculated beginning with the 1998 survey results.

more likely to be Internet users than others. Individuals living in low-income households or having little education, still trail the national average. However, broad measures of Internet use in the United States suggest that over time Internet use has become more equitable (See Chapter 9).

DEMOGRAPHIC FACTORS IN COMPUTER AND INTERNET USE

Income

Family income remains an indicator of whether a person uses a computer or the Internet. Individuals who live in high-income households are more likely to be computer and Internet users than those who live in low-income households. This relationship has held true in each successive survey of computer and Internet use.[6]

Nonetheless, both computer and Internet use have increased steadily across all income categories over time (Figure 2-2). While notable differences remain in Internet use across income categories, Internet use has grown considerably among people who live in lower income households. Among people living in the lowest income households (less than $15,000 annually), Internet use had increased from 9.2 percent in October 1997 to 25.0 percent in September 2001.

---

[6] The individuals who were in a given income bracket in October 1997 are not necessarily the same people in that bracket in September 2001. The family income level of any household changes over time as the income earners make more or less money according to personal and economic circumstances. Thus, the composition of income brackets changes over time.

Figure 2-2: Computer and Internet Use From Any Location by Family Income, Persons Age 3 +

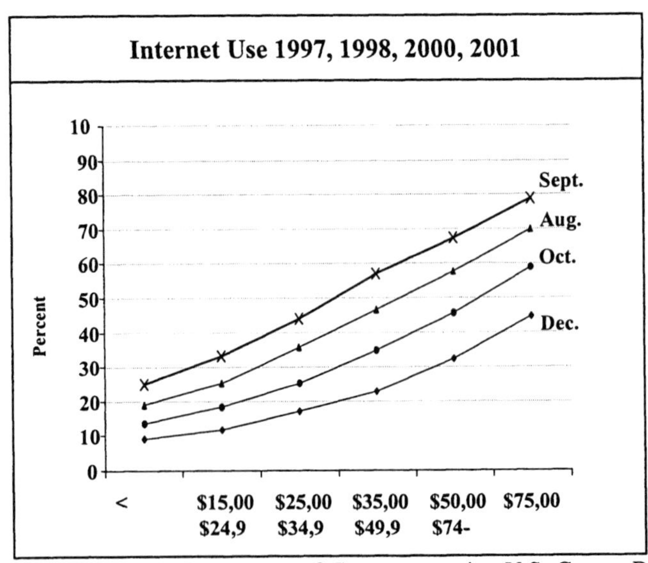

Source: NTIA and ESA, U.S. Department of Commerce, using U.S. Census Bureau Current Population Survey Supplements

Internet use is growing faster among people in lower family income brackets (Figure 2-3, Table 2-3). Internet use among people who live in households where family income is less than $15,000 grew at an annual rate of 25 percent between

December 1998 and September 2001. Over the same period Internet use grew at an annual rate of 11 percent among people living in households where family income was $75,000 or more.

Figure 2-3: Growth in Internet Use by Family Income, Percent of Persons Age 3 + (Annual Rate) December 1998 to September 2001

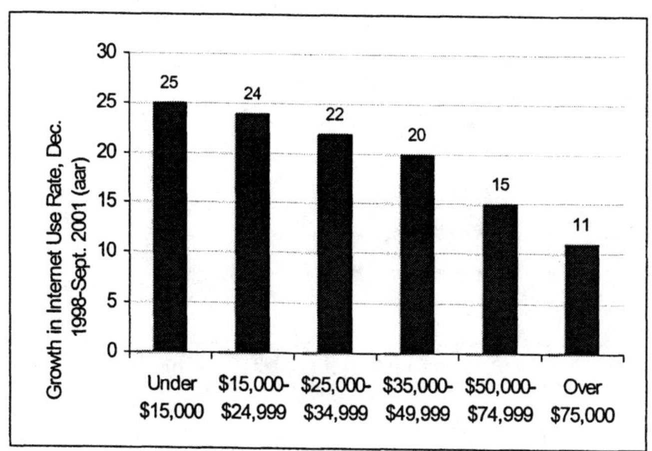

Source: NTIA and ESA, U.S. Department of Commerce, using U.S. Census Bureau Current Population Survey Supplements

Not only did the Internet use rate grow faster for those living in lower income households, but growth also accelerated between August 2000 and September 2001 relative to December 1998 to August 2000. For people living in households in the two lowest income brackets, the Internet use rate grew faster between August 2000 and September 2001 than between December 1998 and August 2000. This acceleration in the growth of Internet use did not occur among people living in higher income households (Table 2-3).

Employment Status

Both the employed and the not employed (either unemployed or not in the labor force) saw growth in computer and Internet use rates since 1997 (Figure 2-4).

Figure 2-4: Computer and Internet Use From Any Location by Employment Status, Percent of Persons Age 16 +

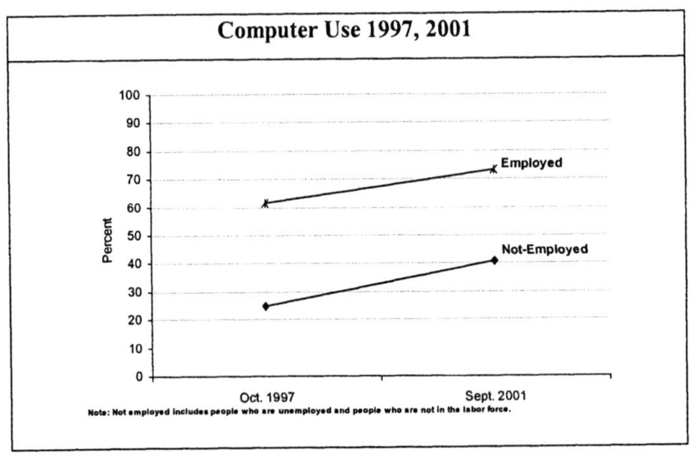

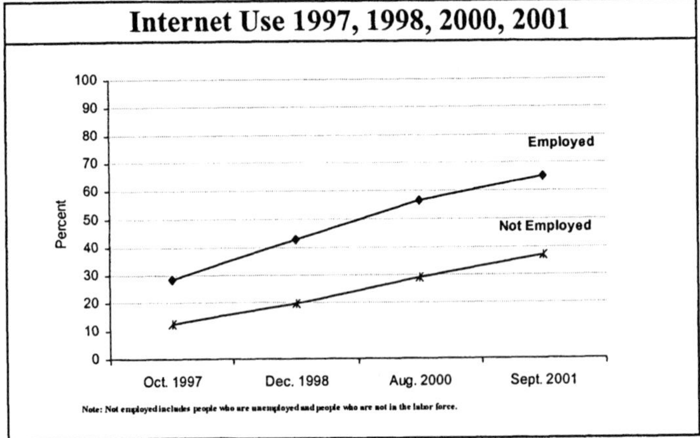

Source: NTIA and ESA, U.S. Department of Commerce, using U.S. Census Bureau Current Population Survey Supplements

People who are employed are more likely to be both computer and Internet users. In 2001, 73.2 percent of employed people (age 16 and older) were computer users and 65.4 percent were Internet users. In contrast, only 40.8 percent of people who were not employed were computer users and 36.9 were Internet users.

Age

Increases in computer and Internet use have occurred across the entire age distribution. Since December 1997, the entire age distribution has shifted upward with each new survey.

Computer and Internet use are strongly associated with the age of the individual. As Figure 2-5 shows, children and teenagers were the most likely to be computer users. Computer use is also relatively high—about 70 percent in 2001—among people in their prime workforce years (generally people in their 20s to their 50s). Those above this age range, are less likely to be computer users. This pattern is consistent in both 1997 and 2001.

Rates of Internet use show a similar pattern that holds true for each year of data. Internet use rates climb steadily as age increases for children through young adults, level off at relatively high rates for people between ages 26 and 55, and then fall among people at higher ages.

Figure 2-5: Computer and Internet Use at Any Location Age Distribution (3 year moving average), Percent of Persons Age 3 to 80

Computer Use 1997, 2001

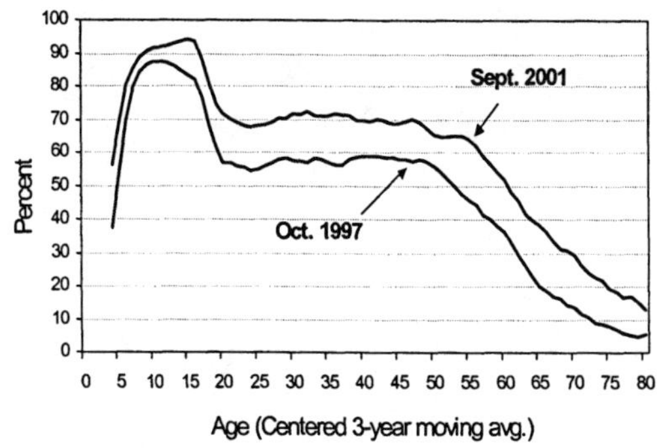

Internet Use 1997, 1998, 2000, 2001

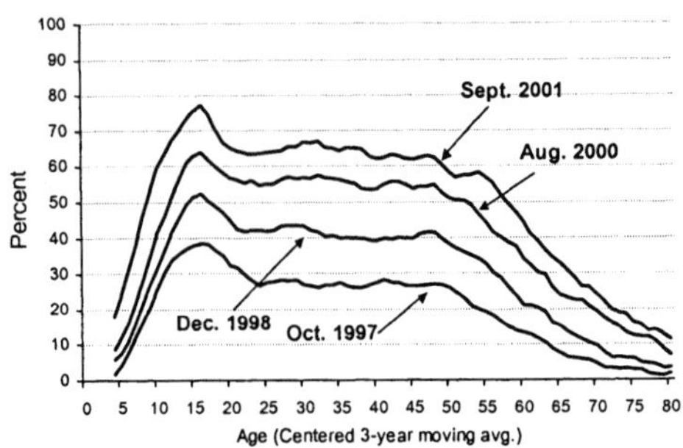

Source: NTIA and ESA, U.S. Department of Commerce, using U.S. Census Bureau Current Population Survey Supplements

One would expect to see the current plateau for Internet use among those age 25 to 55 extend to older ages over time because the overall upward shift in the age distribution shown in Figure 2-5 is composed of two components. The first is an absolute increase in Internet use by people and the second is a cohort effect. The cohort effect describes the fact that the people who are in the 55-year-old age cohort in September 2001 are not the same people who were in this age group in earlier surveys. The 55 year olds of September 2001 were mostly 51 year olds when Census first asked about Internet use in October 1997. People who used the Internet when they were younger will likely continue to do so as they age.

Gender

Males and females have had approximately equal rates of computer use since 1997. In 1997 males were more likely than females to be Internet users. Between October 1997 and August 2000, this difference disappeared. Since August 2000, males and females have had virtually identical rates of Internet use (Figure 2-6). In September 2001, the Internet use rate was 53.9 percent for males and 53.8 percent for females.

The annual growth rates from August 2000 to September 2001 were similar: 19 percent growth at an annual rate for males and 20 percent for females (Table 2-3).

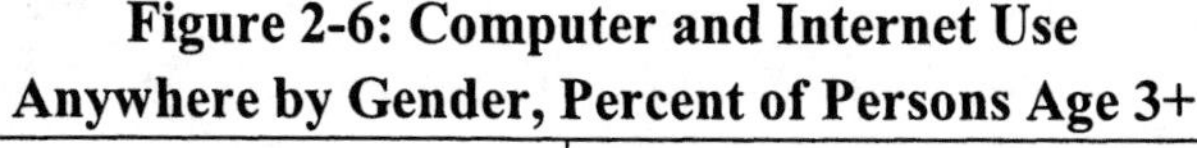

**Figure 2-6: Computer and Internet Use
Anywhere by Gender, Percent of Persons Age 3+**

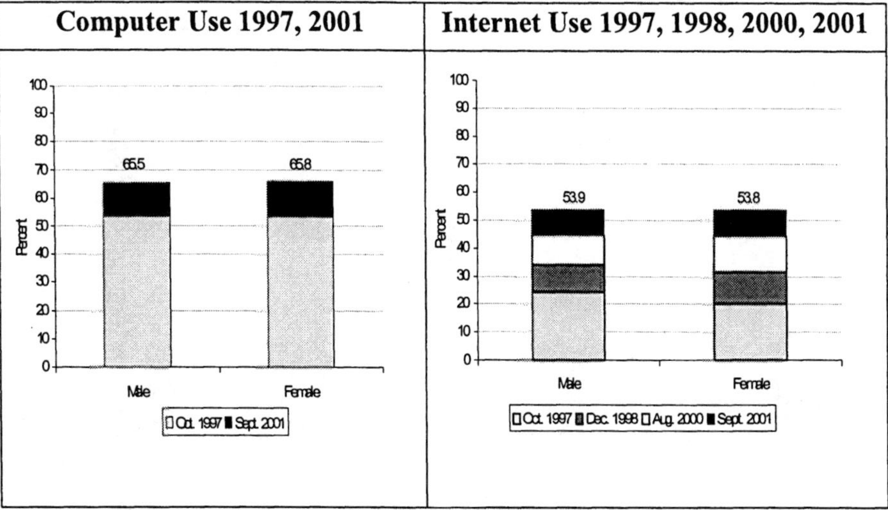

Source: NTIA and ESA, U.S. Department of Commerce, using U.S. Census Bureau Current Population Survey Supplements

Although the aggregate rates of use and growth by gender have equalized, there are still gender-related differences in Internet use within various age groups (Figure 2-7). Women, from approximately age 20 to age 50, are more likely to be Internet users than men. From about age 60 and older, men have higher rates of Internet use than women.

Gender can also be considered in the context of household type.[7] In previous years people who lived in single parent households (where children under the age of 18 are present) headed by women were less likely to be Internet users. The Internet use rate among people living in female-headed single parent households grew dramatically between August 2000 and September 2001, and the differential between Internet use rates between people living in male and female single parent households has largely disappeared.

---

[7] *"Household*. A household consists of all persons--related family members and all unrelated persons--who occupy a housing unit and have no other usual address. A house, an apartment, a group of rooms, or a single room is regarded as a housing unit when occupied or intended for occupancy as separate living quarters. A *householder* is the person (or one of the persons) in whose name the housing unit is owned or rented. *Family*. A family is defined as a group of two or more persons residing together who are related by birth, marriage, or adoption; all such persons are considered as members of one family. Families are classified either as married-couple families or as families maintained by women or men without spouses. A family maintained by a woman or a man is one in which the householder is either single, widowed, divorced, or married, spouse absent." *Current Population Survey Concepts*, (http://www.bls.census.gov/cps/bconcept.htm).

Figure 2-7: Computer and Internet Use Distribution by Age & Gender, Sept. 2001, Percent of Persons Age 3 to 80

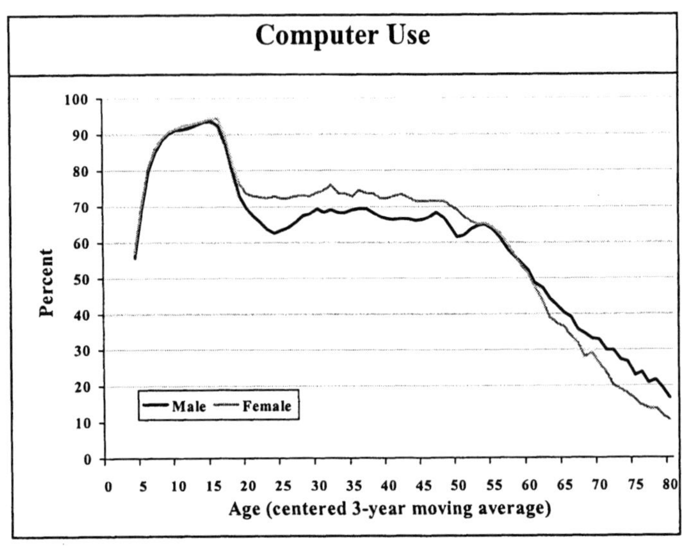

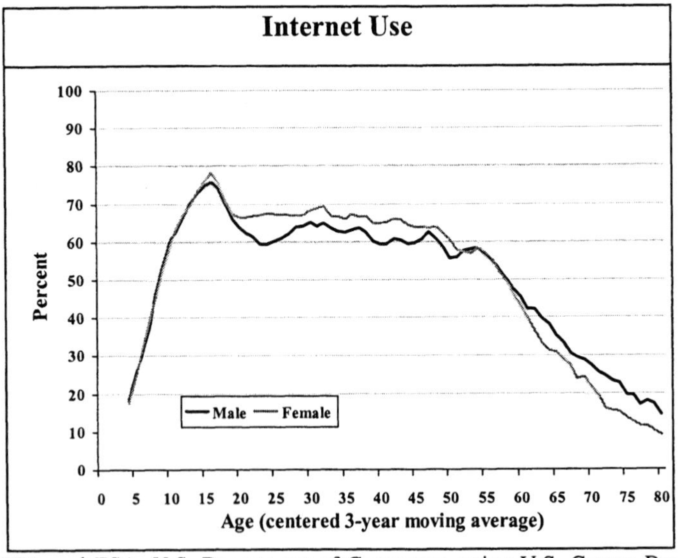

Source: NTIA and ESA, U.S. Department of Commerce, using U.S. Census Bureau Current Population Survey Supplements

However, as Figure 2-8 shows, people who live in households headed by married couples (where children under the age of 18 are present) are more likely than people who live in other household types to be both computer and Internet users.

Figure 2-8: Computer and Internet Use Anywhere by Type of Household, Persons Age 3 +

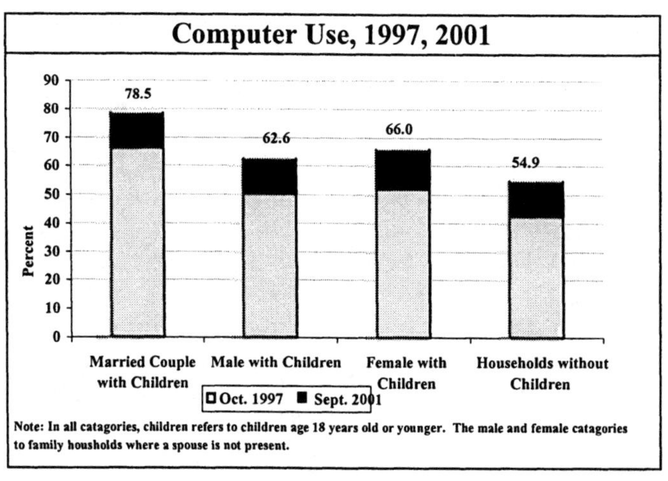

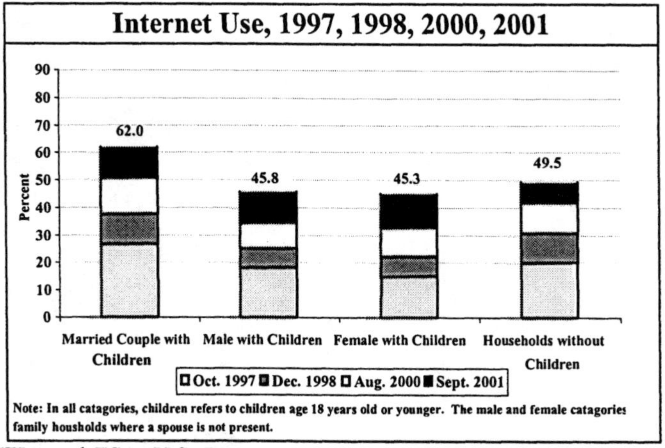

Source: NTIA and ESA, U.S. Department of Commerce, using U.S. Census Bureau Current Population Survey Supplements

Educational Attainment

Educational attainment also factors into computer and Internet use. The higher a person's level of education, the more likely he or she will be a computer or Internet user.

As shown in Figure 2-9, adults (age 25 and above) with education beyond college were the most likely to be both computer and Internet users each year of the survey.[8] Those with Bachelor's degrees trailed close behind. At the opposite end of the spectrum are those adults whose highest level of education is less than high school. In September 2001, the computer use rate for the latter was 17.0 percent and the Internet use rate was 12.8.

Internet use has grown rapidly among those with lower levels of educational attainment. Internet use for adults with a Bachelor's degree and adults with beyond a Bachelor's degree grew at annual rates of 13 and 9 percent, respectively from December 1998 to September 2001. Internet use among those with only a high school diploma grew at an annual rate of 30 percent over the same period (Table 2-3).

Figure 2-9: Internet Use Anywhere by Educational Attainment, Percent of Persons Age 25 +

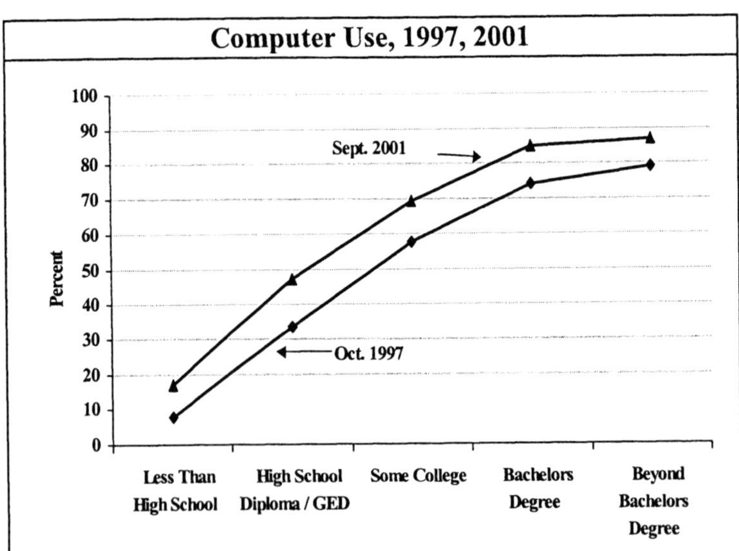

---

[8] Educational attainment is shown for people age 25 and older to reduce the likelihood that the individual is still in school.

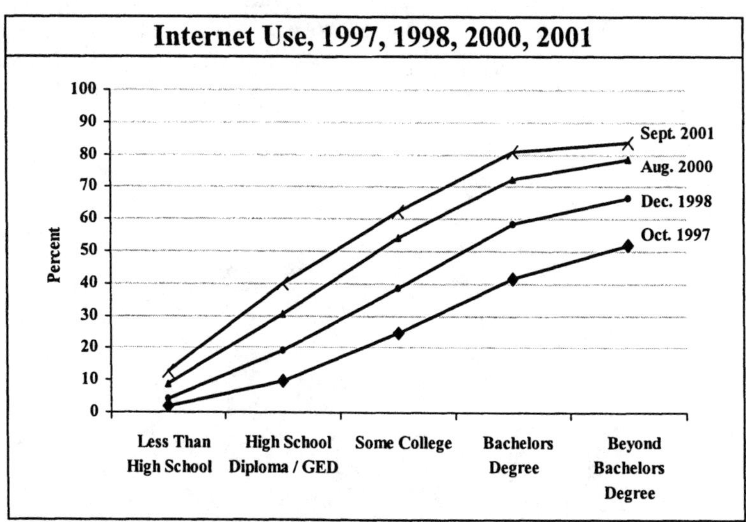

Source: NTIA and ESA, U.S. Department of Commerce, using U.S. Census Bureau Current Population Survey Supplements

Box 2-1: Interrelated Demographic Factors

Descriptive statistics, such as those in this chapter, are not sufficient to determine why a certain group of individuals has higher or lower rates of computer and Internet use. One of the reasons is that demographic characteristics are often interrelated.

An individual's occupation (which is discussed in chapter 6) is often associated with a certain level of education. People with higher incomes often have higher levels of education. Thus, the statistics describing how people living in low income households, or who have low levels of education, or a given occupation are less likely to be Internet users may be capturing a more complicated interaction between the demographic characteristics. For example, income and education are strongly correlated. Thus, the relationship between Internet use and educational attainment could simply reflect the fact that people with higher levels of education tend to have higher incomes.

On closer examination, however, we find that income and education have independent effects on Internet use. Figure 2-10 shows the Internet use rates for each of six income categories broken into four levels of educational attainment. Thus, the entire population 25 years of age or more is assigned to one of 24 income/education categories. As Figure 2-10 shows, people who have lower levels of education but live in households with a high family incomes are less likely to be Internet users than those who have high levels of education and live in households with low family income.

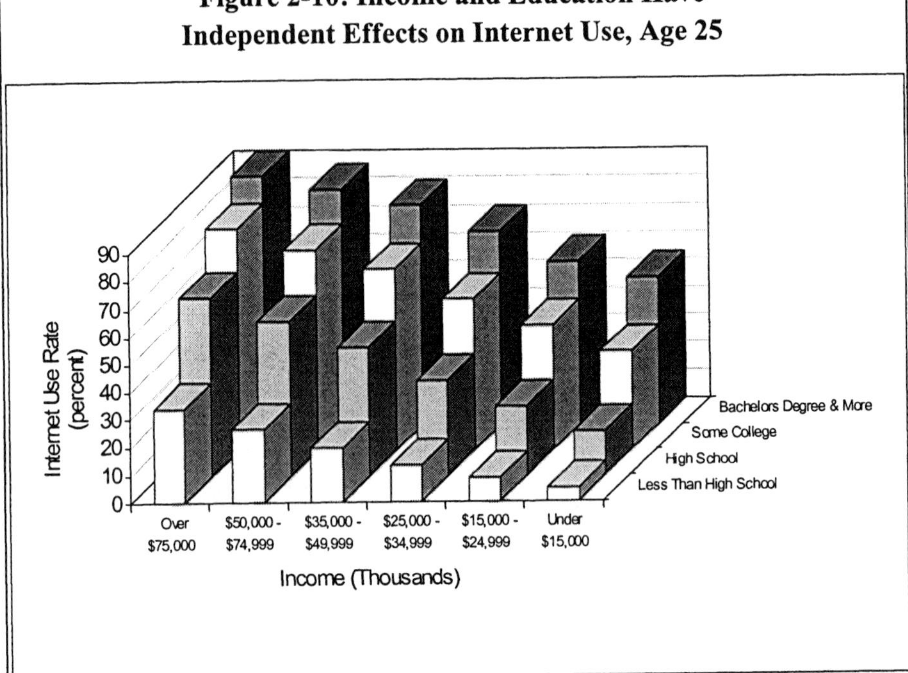

Source: NTIA and ESA, U.S. Department of Commerce, using U.S. Census Bureau Current Population Survey Supplements

Both higher income and more education are themselves correlated with occupations that tend to have greater Internet use at work. As Chapter 6 demonstrates, a person's use at work has an important relationship to whether the Internet is at home, independent of income.

Urban or Rural Location of the Household

In September 2001, people living in each urban/rural category—non-central city urban, central city urban, and rural—had higher rates of Internet use than in previous years[9] (Figure 2-11).

---

[9] The "urban" category includes those areas classified as being urbanized (having a population density of at least 1,000 persons per square mile and a total population of at least 50,000) as well as cities, villages, boroughs (except in Alaska and New York), towns (except in the six New England states, New York, and Wisconsin), and other designated census areas having 2,500 or more persons. A "central city" is the largest city within a "metropolitan" area, as defined by the Census Bureau. Additional cities within the metropolitan area can also be classified as central cities if they meet certain employment, population,

Figure 2-11: Internet Use Anywhere by Geographic Location of Household, Percent of Persons Age 3 +, Sept. 2001

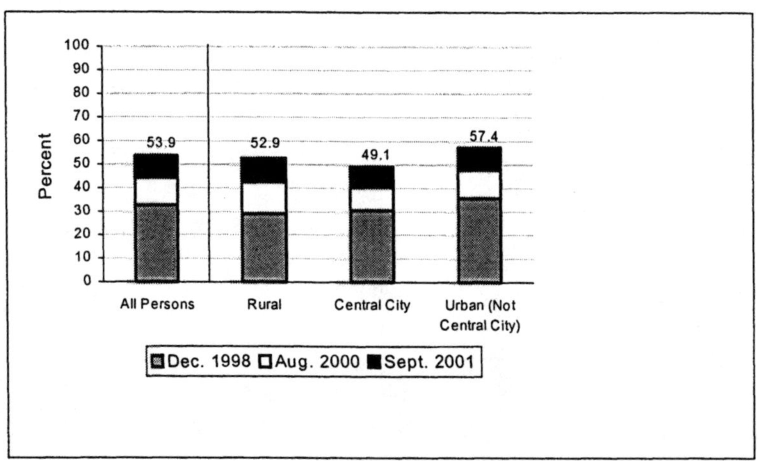

Source: NTIA and ESA, U.S. Department of Commerce, using U.S. Census Bureau Current Population Survey Supplements

Over the 1998 to 2001 period, growth in Internet use among people living in rural households has been particularly strong (24 percent at an average annual rate). Use of the Internet by people in rural households now approaches the national average (Table 2-3). Internet use among people living in central city urban households has also grown, although not as rapidly (19 percent at an average annual rate). Internet use among people who live in non-central city urban households has grown at a slightly slower rate (18 percent at an average annual rate). Even with the slowest growth rate, however, people living in non-central city urban households used the Internet at a rate greater than the other two geographic categories in September 2001.

and employment/residence ratio requirements. "Urban, not central city" equals the "urban" category less the "central city" category. All areas not classified by the Census Bureau as urban are defined as rural and generally include communities of less than 2,500 persons.

Race / Hispanic Origin

Since 1997, rates of computer and Internet use by individuals have increased for each broad race/ethnic category.[10]

Differences in computer and Internet use across these broad race and Hispanic origin categories persist. In each survey, Whites and Asian American Pacific Islanders have had higher rates of both computer and Internet use than Blacks and Hispanics[11] (Figure 2-12, Table 2-2). In September 2001, the computer use rates were highest for Asian American /Pacific Islanders (71.2 percent) and Whites (70.0 percent). Among Blacks, 55.7 percent were computer users. Almost half of Hispanics (48.8 percent) were computer users. During the same year, Internet use among Whites and Asian American/Pacific Islanders hovered around 60 percent, while Internet use rates for Blacks (39.8 percent) and Hispanics (31.6 percent) trailed behind.

On the other hand, Internet use has increased across all race and ethnic groups and growth in Internet use rates was faster for Blacks and Hispanics than for Whites and Asian American/Pacific Islanders (Table 2-3). From December 1998 to September 2001, Internet use among Blacks grew at an annual rate of 31 percent. Internet use among Hispanics grew at an annual rate of 26 percent. Internet use continued to grow among Asian American/Pacific Islanders (21 percent), and Whites (19 percent), although not so rapidly as for Blacks and Hispanics. Although not so dramatic, Blacks and Hispanics also have had somewhat faster growth in computer use than Whites and Asian American/Pacific Islanders (Table 2-1).

Growth in Internet use rates for Blacks and Hispanics also accelerated in the 2000 to 2001 period. Between August 2000 and September 2001, growth in Hispanic Internet use increased to 30 percent from the 24 percent annual rate of growth from December 1998 to August 2000. Growth in Internet use among Blacks increased to a 33 percent annual rate between August 2000 and September 2001, from the 30 percent annual rate of growth between December 1998 and August 2000. Growth rates among Whites and Asian American Pacific Islanders were comparable during both periods.

---

[10] The Current Population Survey is designed primarily to measure accurately national employment on a monthly basis. The survey design is such that measures for certain sub-populations are also accurate. However, this is not the case for all sub-populations. Although the survey includes questions to identify the race/ethnic category "American Indian Alaska Native," the survey design is such that data for this sub-population is unreliable. This category is therefore not reported in this analysis.

[11] Persons categorized as Hispanic are those who indicated that their origin was Mexican-American, Chicano, Mexican, Puerto Rican, Cuban, Central or South American, or other Hispanic. People of Hispanic origins can be of any race. People who have indicated that they are of Hispanic origin are grouped as Hispanic and excluded from the race categories. Thus, "Whites" should be read as "Whites, non-Hispanic" and "Blacks" should be read as "Blacks, non-Hispanic."

Figure 2-12: Internet Use Anywhere by
Race/Hispanic Origin, Percent of Persons Age 3 +

Computer Use 1997, 2001

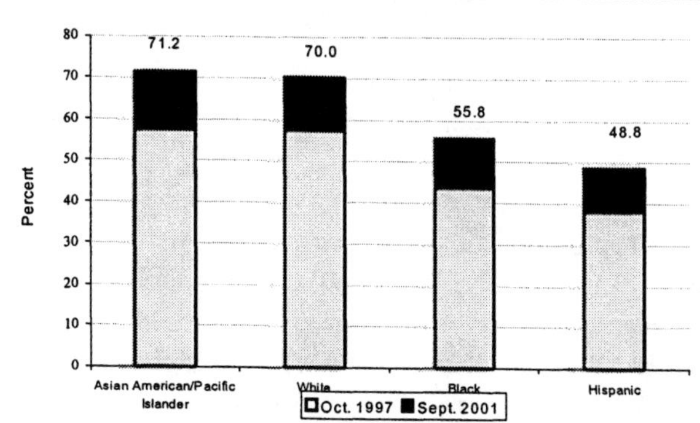

Internet Use 1997, 1998, 2000, 2001

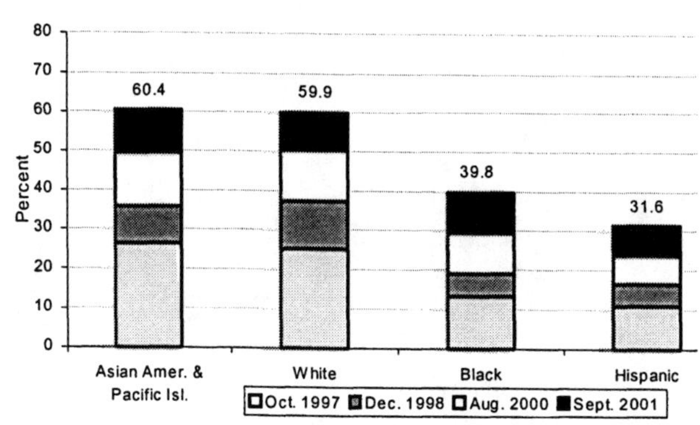

Source: NTIA and ESA, U.S. Department of Commerce, using U.S. Census Bureau Current Population Survey Supplements

The race and ethnic origin categories used in this analysis are broad aggregations of what can be very disparate sub-groups. Individual sub-groups may have higher or lower levels of Internet use than the aggregate. Box 2-2 provides an example of a sub-group of the Hispanic population (those not speaking English in the home) that has much lower levels of Internet use than the aggregate Hispanic population. It is likely that each broad category has sub-groups with rates of computer and Internet use that differ dramatically from the aggregate.

Box 2-2: Example of Differential Internet
Use in a Race/Ethnic Origin Sub-Group

Internet use among Hispanics differs considerably depending on whether Spanish is the only language spoken in the household, which is the case for about one in nine of Hispanic households.[12] In September 2001, 14.1 percent of Hispanics who lived in households where Spanish was the only language spoken used the Internet. In contrast, 37.6 percent of Hispanics who lived in households where Spanish was not the only language spoken used the Internet.

The forces influencing Internet use for these two sub-groups of the Hispanic category are not necessarily clear-cut. One could point to metrics that suggest a predominance of English language sites on the Internet. The Organization for Economic Cooperation and Development, for example, reports that more than 94 percent of links to pages on secure servers were in English in July 2000.[13] Yet, this metric reflects only one use of the Internet—commerce—and provides no information on how much of other Internet traffic (e-mail and other online communications) is English only.

Furthermore, there can be considerable demographic differences among sub-groups. For example, individuals living in Spanish language-only households are more likely to have lower family incomes than those who live in non-Spanish language-only households. The income distribution of individuals living in Spanish language-only households is in fact strikingly different from that for other Hispanics and from the overall income distribution (Figure 2-14). Levels of educational attainment for individuals living in the Spanish-only households also differ from non-Spanish only Hispanic households and other households.

---

[12] The Current Population Survey asks the question "Is Spanish the only language spoken by all members of the household who are 15 years of age or older?" Although this phrasing is restrictive, because it excludes households where Spanish may be the predominant rather than the exclusive language spoken in a household, the results suggest ways in which the aggregate results for people claiming membership in the "Hispanic" ethnic category mask a variety of experiences in using the Internet.

[13] Organization for Economic Cooperation and Development, *Understanding the Digital Divide*, 2001. p.23. (www1.oecd.org/dsti/sti/prod/digital_divide.pdf)

Figure 2-13: The Spanish Only Sub-Groups of the Hispanic Category Have a Strikingly Different Income Distribution than other Hispanics and the Population at Large

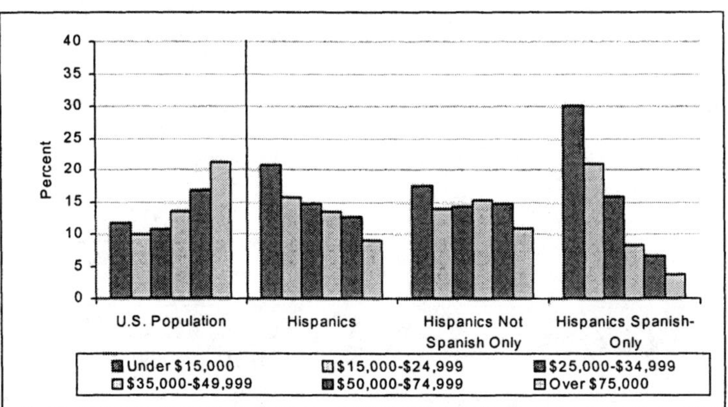

Source: NTIA and ESA, U.S. Department of Commerce, using U.S. Census Bureau Current Population Survey Supplements.

Table 2-1: Computer Use From Any Location by Individuals Age 3 and Older, October 1997 & September 2001

	October 1997		September 2001		Percent of People Who Are Computer Users		Growth in Use Rate (annual rate)
	Computer Users*	Total*	Computer Users*	Total*	Oct. 1997	Sept. 2001	Oct. 1997 to Sept. 2001
Total Population	136,900	255,689	174,051	265,180	53.5	65.6	5.3
Gender							
Male	66,978	124,590	84,539	129,152	53.8	65.5	5.2
Female	69,921	131,099	89,512	136,028	53.3	65.8	5.5
Race/ Origin							
White	105,957	184,295	130,848	186,793	57.5	70.0	5.2
Black	13,854	31,786	18,544	33,305	43.6	55.7	6.5
Asian Amer. & Pac. Isl.	5,306	9,225	7,600	10,674	57.5	71.2	5.6
Hispanic	10,729	28,233	15,690	32,146	38.0	48.8	6.6
Employment Status							
Employed[a]	80,687	130,857	98,819	135,089	61.7	73.2	4.5
Not Employed[a, b]	18,074	72,911	31,487	77,268	24.8	40.8	13.5
Family Income							

	October 1997		September 2001		Percent of People Who Are Computer Users		Growth in Use Rate (annual rate)
	Computer Users*	Total*	Computer Users*	Total*	Oct. 1997	Sept. 2001	Oct. 1997 to Sept. 2001
Less than $15,000	13,182	44,284	11,681	31,354	29.8	37.3	5.9
$15,000 - $24,999	12,115	32,423	12,464	26,649	37.4	46.8	5.9
$25,000 - $34,999	16,360	33,178	16,495	28,571	49.3	57.7	4.1
$35,000 - $49,999	23,440	38,776	25,233	36,044	60.4	70.0	3.8
$50,000 - $74,999	30,043	41,910	35,465	44,692	71.7	79.4	2.6
$75,000 & above	29,542	36,572	49,672	56,446	80.8	88.0	2.2
Educational Attainment							
Less Than High School [c]	2,331	29,114	4,672	27,484	7.9	17.0	21.5
High School Diploma / GED [c]	19,256	57,487	27,118	57,386	33.5	47.3	9.2
Some College [c]	24,595	42,544	31,551	45,420	57.8	69.5	4.8
Bachelors Degree [c]	20,640	27,795	25,965	30,588	74.3	84.9	3.5
Beyond Bachelors Degree [c]	10,970	13,863	14,151	16,283	79.1	86.9	2.4
Age Group							
Age 3 – 8	14,412	24,445	16,877	23,763	59.0	71.0	4.9
Age 9 – 17	30,188	35,469	34,356	37,118	85.1	92.6	2.2
Age 18 – 24	14,528	24,973	19,361	27,137	58.2	71.3	5.3
Age 25 – 49	58,745	101,853	71,491	101,890	57.7	70.2	5.1
Male	27,577	50,177	33,647	50,020	55.0	67.3	5.3
Female	31,168	51,676	37,844	51,871	60.3	73.0	5.0
Age 50 +	19,026	68,949	31,965	75,272	27.6	42.5	11.6
Male	9,654	31,252	15,547	34,438	30.9	45.1	10.2
Female	9,372	37,697	16,418	40,834	24.9	40.2	13.1
Household Type In Which the Individual Lives [d]							
Married Couple w/Children <18 Years Old	68,855	103,791	81,897	104,337	66.3	78.5	4.4
Male Householder w/Children <18 Years Old	3,163	6,284	4,632	7,400	50.3	62.6	5.7
Female Householder w/Children <18 Years Old	14,288	27,327	19,160	29,032	52.3	66.0	6.1
Family Household without Children <18 Years Old	33,001	77,612	46,400	81,996	42.5	56.6	7.6
Non-Family Household	16,589	39,381	21,913	42,333	42.1	51.8	5.4

Source: U.S. Bureau of the Census, Current Population Survey supplements, October, September 2001.

Notes: [a] Age 16 and older. [b] Unemployed and not in the labor force. [c] Age 25 and older. [d] Excludes group quarters, such as dorms and military barracks.

Table 2-2: Internet Use From Any Location by Individuals Age 3 and Older, October 1997, December 1998, August 2000, and September 2001

	Oct. 1997 (thousands)		Dec. 1998 (thousands)		Aug. 2000 (thousands)		Sept. 2001 (thousands)		Internet Use (percent)			
	Internet Users	Total	Internet Users	Total	Internet Users	Total	Internet Users	Total	Oct. 1997	Dec. 1998	Aug. 2000	Sept. 2001
Total Population	56,774	255,689	84,587	258,453	116,480	262,620	142,823	265,180	22.2	32.7	44.4	53.9
Gender												
Male	30,311	124,590	43,033	125,932	56,962	127,844	69,580	129,152	24.3	34.2	44.6	53.9
Female	26,464	131,099	41,555	132,521	59,518	134,776	73,243	136,028	20.2	31.4	44.2	53.8
Race/ Origin												
White	46,678	184,295	69,470	184,980	93,714	186,439	111,942	186,793	25.3	37.6	50.3	59.9
Black	4,197	31,786	6,111	32,123	9,624	32,850	13,237	33,305	13.2	19.0	29.3	39.8
Asian Amer. & Pac. Isl.	2,432	9,225	3,467	9,688	5,095	10,324	6,452	10,674	26.4	35.8	49.4	60.4
Hispanic	3,101	28,233	4,897	29,452	7,325	30,918	10,141	32,146	11.0	16.6	23.7	31.6
Employment Status												
Employed[b]	37,254	130,857	56,539	133,119	76,971	136,044	88,396	135,089	28.5	42.5	56.6	65.4
Not Employed[b, d]	9,012	72,911	14,261	73,891	21,321	73,891	28,531	77,268	12.4	19.5	28.9	36.9
Family Income												
Less than $15,000	4,069	44,284	5,170	37,864	6,057	32,096	7,848	31,354	9.2	13.7	18.9	25.0
$15,000 - $24,999	3,760	32,423	5,623	30,581	7,063	27,727	8,893	26,650	11.6	18.4	25.5	33.4
$25,000 - $34,999	5,666	33,178	8,050	31,836	11,054	31,001	12,591	28,571	17.1	25.3	35.7	44.1
$35,000 - $49,999	8,824	38,776	13,528	39,026	16,690	35,867	20,587	36,044	22.8	34.7	46.5	57.1
$50,000 - $74,999	13,552	41,910	19,902	43,776	25,059	43,451	30,071	44,692	32.3	45.5	57.7	67.3
$75,000 & above	16,276	36,572	24,861	42,221	36,564	52,189	44,547	56,446	44.5	58.9	70.1	78.9

	Oct. 1997 (thousands)		Dec. 1998 (thousands)		Aug. 2000 (thousands)		Sept. 2001 (thousands)		Internet Use (percent)			
	Internet Users	Total	Internet Users	Total	Internet Users	Total	Internet Users	Total	Oct. 1997	Dec. 1998	Aug. 2000	Sept. 2001
Educational Attainment												
Less Than High School [a]	516	29,114	1,228	29,039	2,482	28,254	3,506	27,484	1.8	4.2	8.8	12.8
High School Diploma/GED [a]	5,589	57,487	10,961	57,103	17,425	56,889	22,847	57,386	9.7	19.2	30.6	39.8
Some College [a]	10,548	42,544	16,603	43,038	24,201	44,628	28,321	45,420	24.8	38.6	54.2	62.4
Bachelors Degree [a]	11,503	27,795	16,937	28,990	21,978	30,329	24,726	30,588	41.4	58.4	72.5	80.8
Beyond Bachelors Degree [a]	7,195	13,863	9,635	14,518	12,104	15,426	13,633	16,283	51.9	66.4	78.5	83.7
Age Group (and Labor Force)												
Age 3 – 8	1,748	24,445	2,680	24,282	3,671	23,962	6,637	23,763	7.2	11.0	15.3	27.9
Age 9 – 17	11,791	35,469	15,396	35,821	19,579	36,673	25,480	37,118	33.2	43.0	53.4	68.6
Age 18 – 24	7,884	24,973	11,356	25,662	15,039	26,458	17,673	27,137	31.6	44.3	56.8	65.0
Age 25 – 49	27,639	101,853	41,694	101,836	56,433	101,946	65,138	101,890	27.1	40.9	55.4	63.9
Male	14,679	50,177	20,889	50,054	27,078	50,034	30,891	50,020	29.3	41.7	54.1	61.8
Female	12,960	51,676	20,806	51,781	29,356	51,913	34,247	51,871	25.1	40.2	56.5	66.0
Age 50 +	7,712	68,949	13,669	70,852	21,758	73,580	27,895	75,272	11.2	19.3	29.6	37.1
Male	4,560	31,252	7,356	32,248	10,989	33,561	13,757	34,438	14.6	22.8	32.7	39.9
Female	3,152	37,697	6,313	38,604	10,769	40,019	14,138	40,834	8.4	16.4	26.9	34.6
Geographic Location of Household In Which the Individual Lives												
Rural	n/a	n/a	19,274	65,828	28,889	67,980	35,751	67,642	n/a	29.3	42.5	52.9
Urban	n/a	n/a	65,313	192,625	87,591	194,640	107,072	197,537	n/a	33.9	45.0	54.2
Urban Not Central City	n/a	n/a	41,881	116,091	56,773	118,641	69,342	120,724	n/a	36.1	47.9	57.4
Urban Central City	n/a	n/a	23,432	76,534	30,818	75,999	37,730	76,813	n/a	30.6	40.6	49.1

	Oct. 1997 (thousands)		Dec. 1998 (thousands)		Aug. 2000 (thousands)		Sept. 2001 (thousands)		Internet Use (percent)			
	Internet Users	Total	Internet Users	Total	Internet Users	Total	Internet Users	Total	Oct. 1997	Dec. 1998	Aug. 2000	Sept. 2001
Household Type In Which the Individual Lives												
Married Couple w/Children <18 Years Old	27,664	103,791	41,462	110,295	57,122	112,920	64,714	104,337	26.7	37.6	50.6	62.0
Male Householder w/Children <18 Years Old	1,143	6,284	1,995	7,866	2,825	8,186	3,389	7,400	18.2	25.4	34.5	45.8
Female Householder w/Children <18 Years Old	4,041	27,327	6,219	27,877	9,866	30,034	13,140	29,032	14.8	22.3	32.9	45.3
Family Household without Children <18 Years Old	15,240	77,612	21,660	72,155	29,199	70,521	41,397	81,996	19.6	30.0	41.4	50.5
Non-Family Household	8,293	39,381	13,220	40,199	17,442	40,884	20,136	42,333	21.1	32.9	42.7	47.6

[a] Age 25 and older.
[b] Age 16 and Older.
[c] Both people who are unemployed and people not in the labor force.

Source: U.S. Bureau of the Census, Current Population Survey supplements, October 1997,December 1998, August 2000, September 2001.

Table 2-3: Percent Difference and Growth Rates, Internet Use From Any Location by Individuals Age 3 and Older, October 1997, December 1998, August 2000, and September 2001

	Internet Use (percent)				Percentage Point Difference				Growth in Use Rate (annual rate)			
	Oct. 1997*	Dec. 1998	Aug. 2000	Sept. 2001	1997 to 1998*	1998 to 2000	2000 to 2001	1998 to 2001	1997 to 1998*	1998 to 2000	2000 to 2001	1998 to 2001
Total Population	22.2	32.7	44.4	53.9	n/a	11.7	9.5	21.2	n/a	20	20	20
Gender												
Male	24.3	34.2	44.6	53.9	n/a	10.4	9.3	19.7	n/a	17	19	18
Female	20.2	31.4	44.2	53.8	n/a	12.8	9.7	22.5	n/a	23	20	22
Race/ Origin												
White	25.3	37.6	50.3	59.9	n/a	12.7	9.7	22.4	n/a	19	18	19
Black	13.2	19.0	29.3	39.8	n/a	10.3	10.5	20.7	n/a	30	33	31
Asian Amer. & Pac. Isl.	26.4	35.8	49.4	60.4	n/a	13.6	11.1	24.7	n/a	21	21	21
Hispanic	11.0	16.6	23.7	31.6	n/a	7.1	7.9	15.0	n/a	24	30	26
Employment Status												
Employed[b]	28.5	42.5	56.6	65.4	n/a	14.1	8.9	23.0	n/a	19	14	17
Not Employed[b, d]	12.4	19.5	28.9	36.9	n/a	9.4	8.1	17.4	n/a	27	26	26
Family Income												
Less than $15,000	9.2	13.7	18.9	25.0	n/a	5.2	6.2	11.4	n/a	21	30	25
$15,000 - $24,999	11.6	18.4	25.5	33.4	n/a	7.1	7.9	15.0	n/a	22	28	24
$25,000 - $34,999	17.1	25.3	35.7	44.1	n/a	10.4	8.4	18.8	n/a	23	22	22
$35,000 - $49,999	22.8	34.7	46.5	57.1	n/a	11.9	10.6	22.5	n/a	19	21	20
$50,000 - $74,999	32.3	45.5	57.7	67.3	n/a	12.2	9.6	21.8	n/a	15	15	15
$75,000 & above	44.5	58.9	70.1	78.9	n/a	11.2	8.9	20.0	n/a	11	12	11

	Internet Use (percent)				Percentage Point Difference				Growth in Use Rate (annual rate)			
	Oct. 1997*	Dec. 1998	Aug. 2000	Sept. 2001	1997 to 1998*	1998 to 2000	2000 to 2001	1998 to 2001	1997 to 1998*	1998 to 2000	2000 to 2001	1998 to 2001
Educational Attainment												
Less Than High School [a]	1.8	4.2	8.8	12.8	n/a	4.6	4.0	8.5	n/a	55	41	49
High School Diploma / GED [a]	9.7	19.2	30.6	39.8	n/a	11.4	9.2	20.6	n/a	32	27	30
Some College [a]	24.8	38.6	54.2	62.4	n/a	15.7	8.1	23.8	n/a	23	14	19
Bachelors Degree [a]	41.4	58.4	72.5	80.8	n/a	14.0	8.4	22.4	n/a	14	11	13
Beyond Bachelors Degree [a]	51.9	66.4	78.5	83.7	n/a	12.1	5.3	17.4	n/a	11	6	9
Age Group (and Labor Force)												
Age 3 – 8	7.2	11.0	15.3	27.9	n/a	4.3	12.6	16.9	n/a	22	74	40
Age 9 – 17	33.2	43.0	53.4	68.6	n/a	10.4	15.3	25.7	n/a	14	26	19
Age 18 – 24	31.6	44.3	56.8	65.0	n/a	12.6	8.5	21.0	n/a	16	13	15
Age 25 – 49	27.1	40.9	55.4	63.9	n/a	14.4	8.6	23.0	n/a	20	14	18
Male	29.3	41.7	54.1	61.8	n/a	12.4	7.6	20.0	n/a	17	13	15
Female	25.1	40.2	56.5	66.0	n/a	16.4	9.5	25.8	n/a	23	15	20
Age 50 +	11.2	19.3	29.6	37.1	n/a	10.3	7.5	17.8	n/a	29	23	27
Male	14.6	22.8	32.7	39.9	n/a	9.9	7.2	17.1	n/a	24	20	23
Female	8.4	16.4	26.9	34.6	n/a	10.6	7.7	18.3	n/a	35	26	31
Geographic Location of Household In Which the Individual Lives												
Rural	n/a	29.3	42.5	52.9	n/a	13.2	10.4	23.6	n/a	25	22	24
Urban	n/a	33.9	45.0	54.2	n/a	11.1	9.2	20.3	n/a	19	19	19
Urban Not Central City	n/a	36.1	47.9	57.4	n/a	11.8	9.6	21.4	n/a	18	18	18
Urban Central City	n/a	30.6	40.6	49.1	n/a	9.9	8.6	18.5	n/a	18	19	19

	Internet Use (percent)				Percentage Point Difference				Growth in Use Rate (annual rate)			
	Oct. 1997*	Dec. 1998	Aug. 2000	Sept. 2001	1997 to 1998*	1998 to 2000	2000 to 2001	1998 to 2001	1997 to 1998*	1998 to 2000	2000 to 2001	1998 to 2001
Household Type In Which the Individual Lives												
Married Couple w/Children <18 Years Old	26.7	37.6	50.6	62.0	n/a	13.0	11.4	24.4	n/a	20	21	20
Male Householder w/Children <18 Years Old	18.2	25.4	34.5	45.8	n/a	9.1	11.3	20.4	n/a	20	30	24
Female Householder w/Children <18 Years Old	14.8	22.3	32.9	45.3	n/a	10.5	12.4	23.0	n/a	26	34	29
Household Type In Which the Individual Lives												
Family Household without Children <18 Years Old	19.6	30.0	41.4	50.5	n/a	11.4	9.1	20.5	n/a	21	20	21
Non-Family Household	21.1	32.9	42.7	47.6	n/a	9.8	4.9	14.7	n/a	17	11	14

* The October 1997 question on Internet use was worded considerably differently than the questions used in the following years. The use rates calculated from the October 1997 data are likely correct in terms of their order of magnitude. Growth rates have, however, not been calculated because the implied precision of the year-to-year comparisons would be inaccurate.

[a] Age 25 and older.

[b] Age 16 and Older.

[c] Both people who are unemployed and people not in the labor force.

Source: U.S. Bureau of the Census, Current Population Survey supplements, October 1997, December 1998, August 2000, September 2001.

Chapter 3

ONLINE ACTIVITIES

As an increasing number of Americans are going online, they are engaging in a wide variety of online activities. Nearly half (45.0 percent) of the population now uses e-mail. The September 2001 survey asked respondents to report on activities in sixteen areas, compared to the nine activities measured in the August 2000 survey. This year's survey revealed that activity levels for the original nine categories continued to grow, while also reporting strong activity levels for the newly added categories.

PRIMARY USES BY THE U.S. POPULATION

The chief uses of the Internet remained the same in September 2001 as in August 2000, but occurred at much higher levels (Figure 3-1). The predominant use continued to be e-mail or instant messaging. In September 2001, nearly half of the population used e-mail (45.2 percent, up from 35.4 percent in 2000). Searching for information also ranked high: approximately one-third of Americans used the Internet to search for product and service information (36.2 percent, up from 26.1 percent in 2000), and to search for news, weather, and sports information (33.3 percent, up from 19.2 percent in 2000).

In addition, many more Internet users reported making online purchases or conducting online banking. The August 2000 survey combined these two categories and found that 14.0 percent of online users were engaged in both activities. The September 2001 survey, however, asked about these activities separately and found that 21.0 percent made online purchases and 8.1 percent conducted banking online.

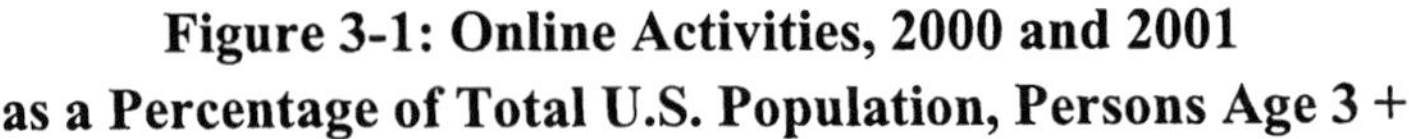

**Figure 3-1: Online Activities, 2000 and 2001
as a Percentage of Total U.S. Population, Persons Age 3 +**

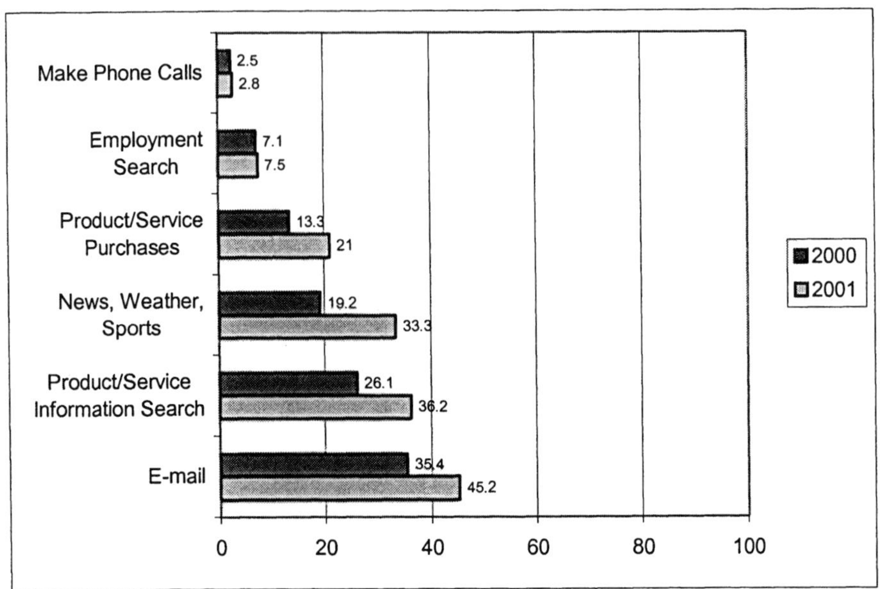

Source: NTIA and ESA, U.S. Department of Commerce, using U.S. Census Bureau Current Population Survey Supplements

ACTIVITIES AMONG THOSE INDIVIDUALS ONLINE

Looking more specifically at *Internet users*, e-mail easily outdistances all other online activity (Figure 3-2). Online users are also connecting to the Internet in large numbers to search for information, whether it is product/services, health, or government services. The Internet is also a source for news and sports for many online users. To the extent that product/service purchases, online trading, and online banking represent consumers engaged in e-commerce, that activity is fairly strong and growing.

Whether an Internet user engages in a certain activity varies by some, but not all, demographic factors. For example, geography has little impact on the selection of activity. The proportions of Internet users engaged in specific online activities varies little across regions, and was similar regardless of whether the Internet user lived in a rural, urban, or central city area. Household type also showed little, if any, differences. Gender, age, race, and income, however, do have some relationship with Internet users' selection of online activities, as discussed below.

**Figure 3-2: Activities of Individuals Online, 2001
as a Percentage of Internet Users, Persons Age 3 +**

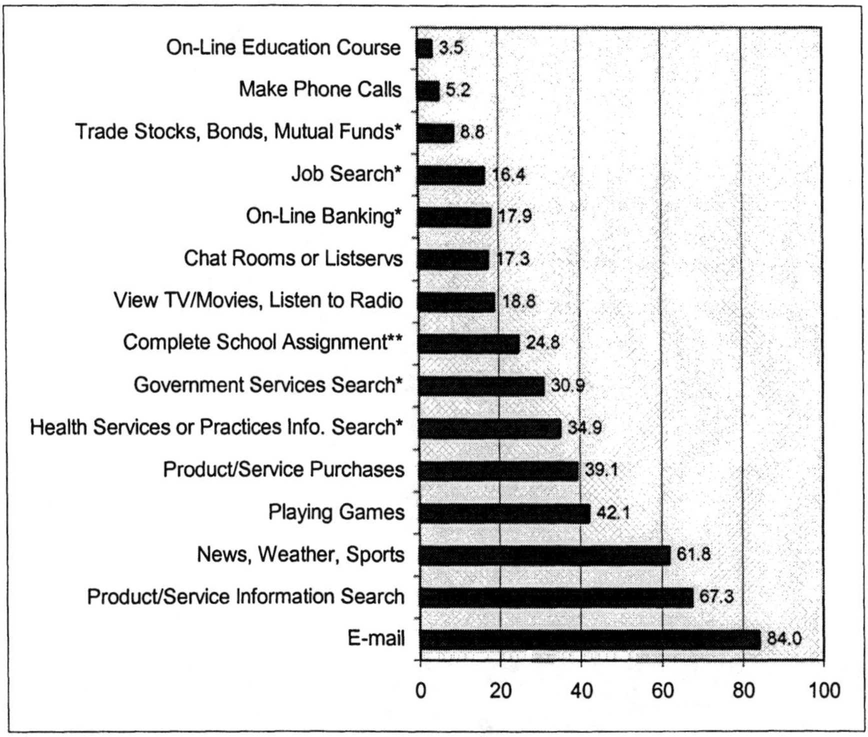

*   These online activities surveyed individuals age 15 and over only.

** This activity was asked of all respondents. If the response was restricted to individuals enrolled in school, the percentage of Internet users completing school assignments would increase to 77.5 percent.

Source: NTIA and ESA, U.S. Department of Commerce, using U.S. Census Bureau Current Population Survey Supplements

Gender

Male and female Internet users engage in some online activities at different rates. More men than women used the Internet to check news, weather, and sports (67.1 percent versus 56.7 percent respectively), but more women went online to find information on health services or practices (39.8 percent contrasted with 29.6 percent for men). A higher proportion of male Internet users use the Internet for financial purposes as compared with females: they were more than twice as likely as females to trade online (12.6 percent of males compared to 5.3 percent of females), and males were slightly more likely to bank online than female users (19.3 percent versus 16.5 percent).

A larger percentage of male Internet users reported using the Internet for entertainment-oriented activities. A higher proportion of males versus females played games online (45.3 percent versus 39.1 percent, respectively) and viewed television or movies or listened to the radio (21.9 percent versus 15.9 percent, respectively).

Men and women responded similarly for the remaining categories surveyed. For example, 82.8 percent of male Internet users e-mailed, compared to 85.1 percent of female Internet users; 16.9 percent of male Internet users searched online for jobs, compared to 16.0 percent of female Internet users; and 18.4 percent of male Internet users participated in online chat rooms or list servs, compared to 16.3 percent of female Internet users.

Age

An Internet user's age also affects online use and activities. Those 55 and older were least likely to use the Internet in many of the surveyed categories, such as playing games, job searching, participating in chat rooms or list servs, viewing television or movies, listening to the radio, or trading online. On the other hand, this age group was more likely (42.7 percent) than any other age group to check health information online. And those 55 and older showed equally strong e-mail use as any other adult age group and by a slight margin to use email.

Internet users in the 25-34 age group were the most likely to bank online (26.1 percent), followed by the Internet users in the 35-44 age group (21.3 percent), the 45-54 age group (17.7 percent) and the 55 and above age group (13.0 percent).

Online shopping is particularly common among 25-34 years old Internet users. About half of the people in this age group (53.0 percent) used the Internet for online shopping, as did 51.2 percent of the 35-44 year olds.

An in depth look at Internet users under the age of 25 is presented in Chapter 5.

**Figure 3-3: Selected Online Activity by Age, 2001
As a Percent of Internet Users, Persons Age 25 +**

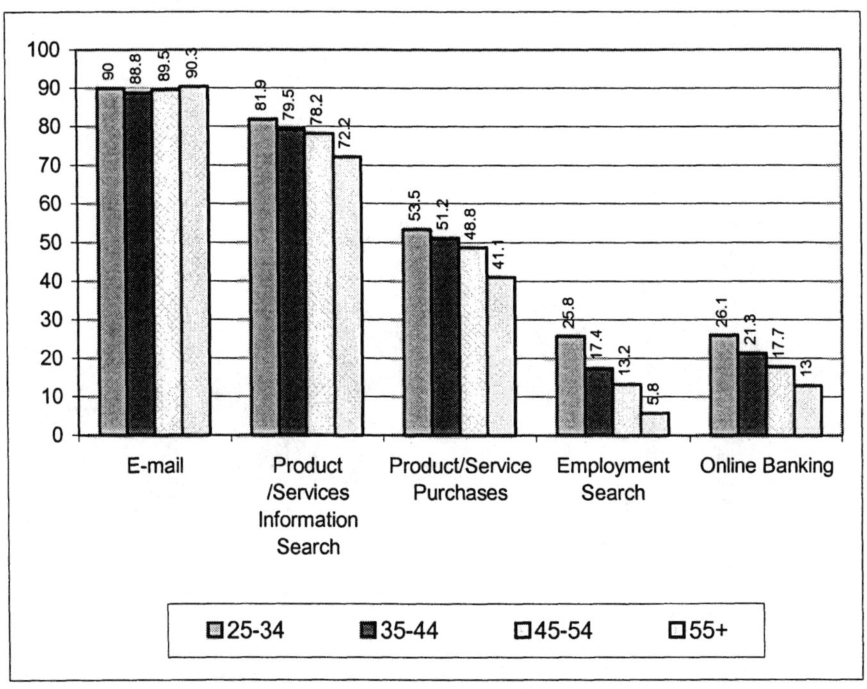

Source: NTIA and ESA, U.S. Department of Commerce, using U.S. Census Bureau Current Population Survey Supplements

Race

Internet users of different racial and Hispanic backgrounds are increasingly using the Internet for a number of online activities. Differences exist among the various racial and Hispanic Internet users regarding their levels of online activities (Figure 3-4). A smaller proportion of Black and Hispanic Internet users email, search for news, conduct searches for product/service information or make online purchases.

**Figure 3-4: Selected Online Activity by Race/Hispanic Origin, 2001
as a Percent of Internet Users, Persons Age 3 +**

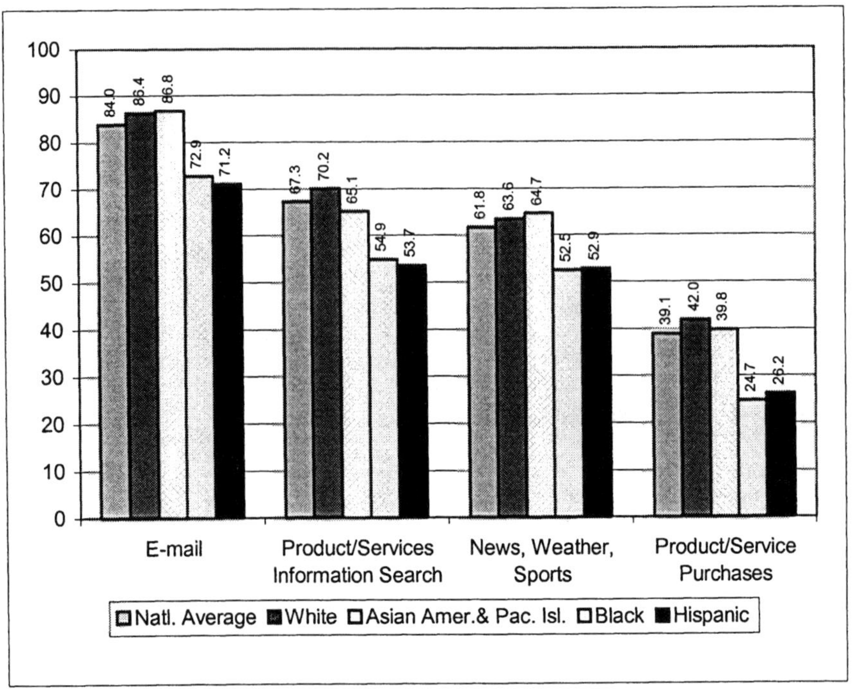

Source: NTIA and ESA, U.S. Department of Commerce, using U.S. Census Bureau Current
Population Survey Supplements

Income

Comparing income levels and online activities reveals a general pattern that shows broader use as income increases. The proportion of Internet users in the highest income level (households earning more than $75,000 a year) exceeds all other income groups in eight of the sixteen online categories surveyed. As demonstrated in Table 3-1, these individuals were more likely to use the Internet to: search for health services or product information, search for government services or agency information, purchase products or services, search for products and services, bank, trade, e-mail or search for news, sports or weather.

Table 3-1: Online Activities of Internet Users by Household Family Income, 20001 Percent of Internet Users Age 3 +

	Under 15,000	15,000-24,999	25,000-34,999	35,000-49,999	50,000-74,999	Over 75,000
E-Mail/Instant Messaging	72.0	75.5	78.7	81.3	85.0	89.1
Playing Games	47.0	48.6	45.7	44.5	42.9	37.5
News, Weather, Sports	53.5	55.5	57.2	58.3	63.2	67.0
Product/Service Information Search	54.9	58.0	63.3	64.2	68.5	73.5
Complete School Assignments	37.1	27.3	25.1	22.9	23.3	24.6
Job Search	23.0	20.6	20.5	17.4	16.0	14.6
Chat Rooms or Listservs	23.0	20.0	18.8	16.9	16.5	16.5
Health Services or Practices. Info. Search	29.5	29.9	32.7	32.9	35.1	38.9
Government Services Search	28.1	27.2	28.0	29.6	29.6	35.1
Product/Service Purchases	26.1	26.8	31.4	35.0	39.4	49.1
View TV/Movies, Listen to Radio	20.0	19.1	19.1	18.6	18.5	19.8
On-Line Banking	12.8	12.1	14.4	15.6	18.0	23.0
On-Line Education Course	4.0	3.2	3.1	3.6	3.5	4.0
Trade Stocks, Bonds, Mutual Funds	3.2	2.9	4.9	6.3	8.1	13.8
Make Phone Calls	6.7	6.3	5.2	5.9	4.8	5.1

Source: NTIA and ESA, U.S. Department of Commerce, using U.S. Census Bureau Current Population Survey Supplements

Chapter 4

HOW AND WHERE AMERICA GOES ONLINE

Internet users are expanding how and where they go online. Faster connection speeds through digital subscriber lines (DSL) and cable are now available to more users as these technologies continue to expand their geographical reach. New devices offer the opportunity for access without a computer and increased mobility of use. Most striking, however, is the growth in the number of people who use the Internet from more than one location.

CONNECTION TYPES: THE EXPANSION OF BROADBAND

Most individuals who use the Internet at home make that connection via a regular "dial up" telephone line (80.0 percent), with cable modems being the second most common way to connect (12.9 percent), followed by DSL (6.6 percent).

Generally referred to as "broadband," cable modems and DSL allow for higher speed access than is available through dial-up.[14] The use of these services in residential settings has rapidly increased over the past year. In August 2000, only 4.0 percent of all individuals or 11.2 percent of home Internet users claimed to have something faster than a dial-up service in their homes. As of September 2001, those

---

[14] This study asked respondents about the two most common broadband technologies available in the United States, digital subscriber line (DSL) and cable modems plus any "other" higher-speed Internet access used at home. These technologies usually feature broadband capabilities, although some applications or connections may possess speeds lower than the 200 kilobits per second—either in both directions or only upstream— that the Federal Communications Commission defines as "full broadband." *See In the Matter of Local Competition and Broadband Reporting,* Report and Order, CC Docket No.99-301 (rel. March 30, 2000) at ¶ 22.

figures had risen to 10.8 percent of the population or 20.0 percent of individuals who use the Internet at home.[15]

**Figure 4-1: Home Internet Connection Type, 2001
as a Percent of Individuals Using the Internet at Home**

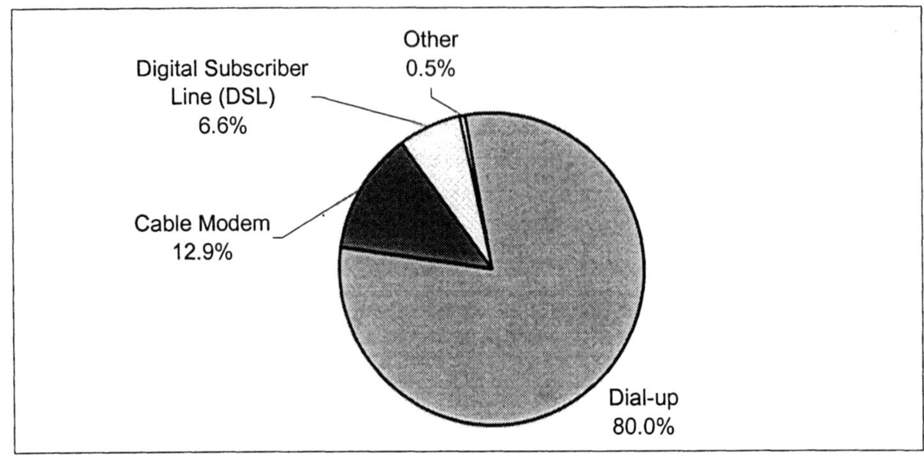

Source: NTIA and ESA, U.S. Department of Commerce, using U.S. Census Bureau Current Population Survey Supplements

This strong growth of approximately 116 percent over a 13-month period coincides with the growing availability of these services. Until very recently, broadband was only available in selected areas of the country. For example, the Federal Communications Commission (FCC) reported that high-speed subscribers were present in 75 percent of the nation's zip codes at the end of December 2000 as compared to 56 percent at the end of 1999. The deployment of broadband occurred first in higher density areas. According to the FCC, high-speed subscribers were present in 97 percent of the most densely populated zip codes at the end of December 2000 as compared to 45 percent of zip codes with the lowest population densities.[16] As shown in Figure 4-2, differences by population density continued to carry over into 2001 with rural areas trailing urban areas and central cities.

---

[15] Homes with broadband have, on average, a higher number of individual Internet users. For example, on a household basis, Internet connection through something other than dial-up increased from 10.7 percent to 19.1 percent between August 2000 and September 2001 among those households with home Internet connection—lower percentages than recorded on an individual basis.

[16] tp://www.fcc.gov/Bureaus/Common_Carrier/News_Releases/2001/nrcc0133.html

**Figure 4-2: Higher-Speed Internet Connection by Geographic Area
as a Percent of Total U.S. Internet Households**

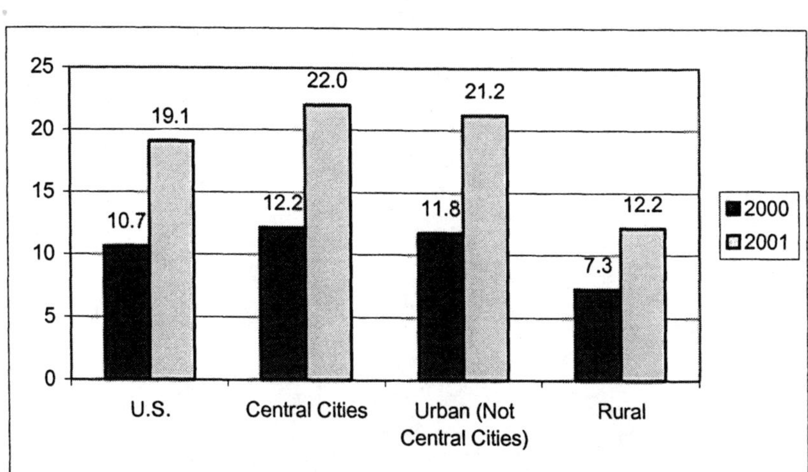

Source: NTIA and ESA, U.S. Department of Commerce, using U.S. Census Bureau Current
Population Survey Supplements

The growth in broadband subscribership compares favorably to the deployment
rates of other communications technologies and services. Broadband deployment
reached 8 percent of U.S. households in early 2001—an adoption speed that outstrips
other technologies such as color television, cell phones, pagers, and VCRs.[17]

Because cable and DSL Internet are more costly than dial-up services, the
proportion of Internet users subscribing to these broadband services varies in expected
ways, with individuals in high-income households, for example, having higher
subscribership rates than individuals in lower income households.

Individuals with broadband access at home had a modestly greater likelihood of
engaging in the activities shown in Figure 3-2. For example, although 84 percent of
Internet users send e-mail, that figure rises to 87 percent for broadband users
specifically. The only activity reflecting a large difference between broadband users
and the Internet-using population, in general, is in the viewing of television or movies
or listening to the radio. In September 2001, 28.2 percent of broadband users engaged
in these activities, compared to 18.8 percent of Internet users generally.

---

[17] Although it uses a different definition of "broadband" than is used in this report, Figure 4-3 provides a
useful illustration of the relative deployment speeds of some familiar communications technologies. See
supra note 14 for discussion of broadband definition.

Figure 4-3: Rate of Deployment of Selected Technologies

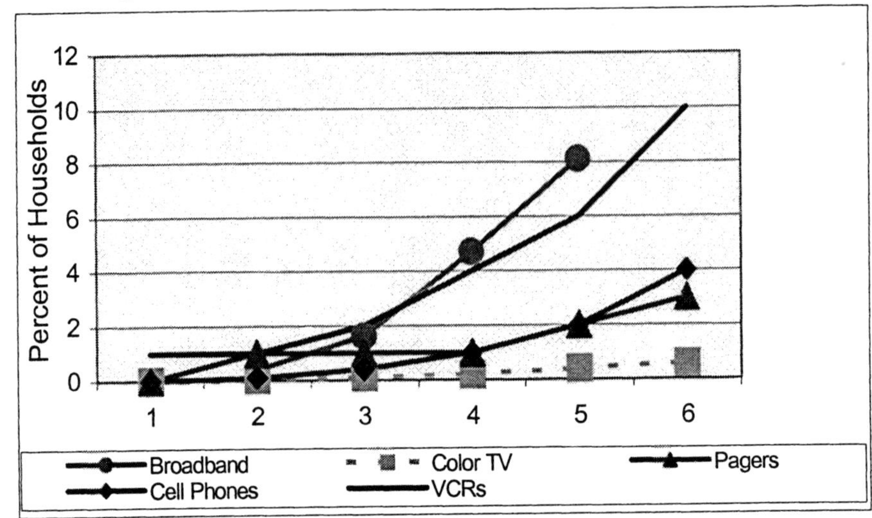

Source: eBrain Market Research and the National Cable and Telecommunications Association

SPREAD OF NEW DEVICES

The vast majority of Internet users in the United States still access the Internet through a desktop or laptop computer.[18] Although the number of people using alternative Internet access devices is increasing, the survey revealed that people who use them typically also have a computer. In September 2001, only 1.5 percent of the households that had home Internet access did not also have a computer.[19]

The only category of alternative Internet access device owned by more than 2 percent of households is Internet-enabled cell phones or pagers (4.8 percent) and virtually all of these households also have computers.[20] Only 1.8 percent of households include a household member who has an Internet accessible personal digital assistant (PDA) or other handheld device, and 0.6 percent of households have Internet access through a television-based system. The television-based systems are the only category

---

[18] This is not universally the case in other countries. In Japan, for example, 30 million people access the Internet through NTT DoCoMo's i-Mode using a handheld device. Although iMode does not have full Internet capability, it is widely used in Japan to access the subset of Internet information available to subscribers. See http://www.NTTdocomo.com.

[19] The questions on Internet access devices were only asked of the household. No information is available on actual use of these devices on a per person basis.

[20] The questions on Internet access devices were asked only of the household. No information is available on actual use of these devices on a paper per person basis.

of alternative access devices where a substantial proportion of subscribing households do not also have a computer (44.4 percent), but this category accounts for 0.6 percent of total households.

LOCATION OF USE

Increased use of mobile Internet devices may eventually make the question of location less important. For now, however, when most access still occurs through less than portable personal computers, where people use the Internet may have implications for the quality of access they enjoy (i.e., the degree of availability or access they actually have) or the type of activities they undertake online.[21] For example, home Internet access may be thought of as a higher quality type of access because it is available (theoretically) 24 hours a day, seven days a week, while school or library access periods are limited to specific hours and often with time limits per session.

As shown in Figure 4-4, the most significant change between December 1998 and September 2001 is the substantial increase in the proportion of people who use the Internet both at home and from some other location.[22] At the end of 1998, only 6.5 percent of the population used the Internet both at home and from some other location. In just under three years, that figure had almost quadrupled to 24.5 percent. That a growing number of people connect from multiple locations could indicate that the Internet is increasingly viewed as a basic communication and information tool, closer in nature to the telephone than the desktop computer.

Figure 4-4 also gives information as to the change in the proportion of the population using the Internet in each category: at home and from some other location. In December 1998, 22.3 percent of the population used the Internet at home (15.8 percent plus 6.5 percent). Home use had grown to 43.6 percent by September 2001. Similarly, Internet use from a location outside the home grew from 17.0 percent to 34.8 percent over the same period.

---

[21] The sample size of households that have Internet-enabled cell phones or pagers, but no computer, is too small for a reliable estimate to be reported.

[22] December 1998 is used as a basis of comparison rather than August 2000. The data from the August 2000 survey reflected the fact that students were generally not in school when the survey took place, and there appeared to be a downward bias on Internet use outside of the home.

Figure 4-4: Internet Use by Location as a Percent of U.S. Population, 1998 and 2001

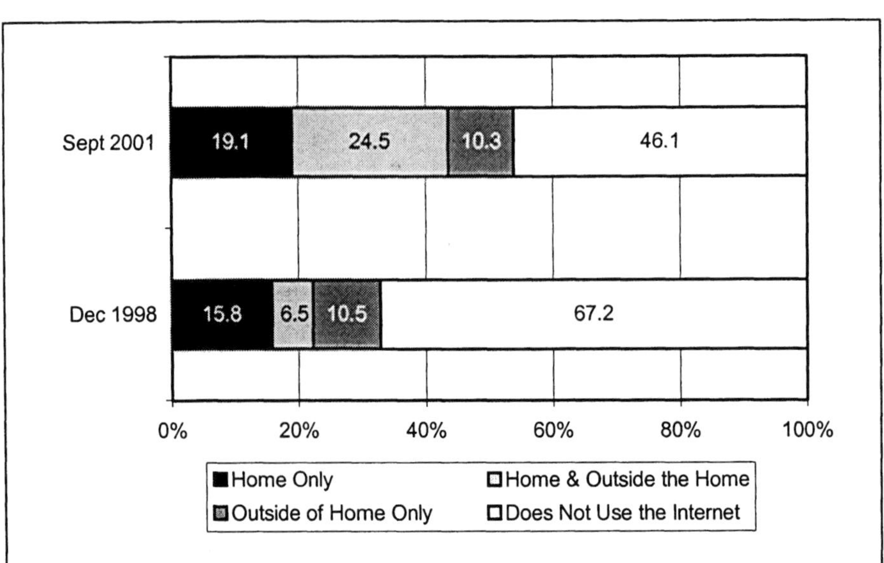

Source: NTIA and ESA, U.S. Department of Commerce, using U.S. Census Bureau Current Population Survey Supplements

"Outside the home" covers a variety of locations. The September 2001 survey asks specifically about Internet use at six locations: work, school, public libraries, community centers, someone else's house, and "somewhere else." Figure 4-5 shows that no single category of "outside the home" comes close to Internet use at home in terms of utilization by a proportion of the U.S. population. However, percent of the total population may not be the most useful basis on which to consider location of use. For example, the 51.9 million people who use the Internet at work represent 19.6 percent of the population, but 38.4 percent of those who work. Similarly, the 31.5 million who use the Internet at school account for only 11.9 percent of the total population, but 44.8 percent who attend school. Chapters 5 and 6 focus specifically on these school and work subgroups.

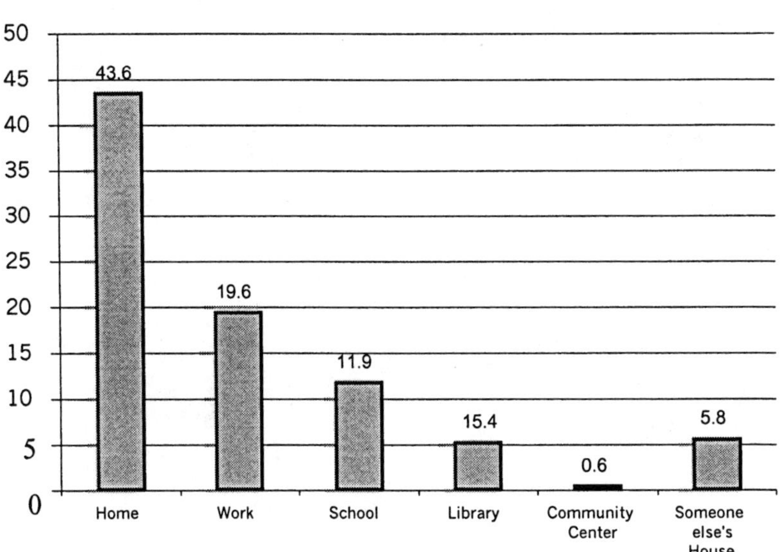

**Figure 4-5: Internet Use by Specific Location
as a Percent of U.S. Population**

Source: NTIA and ESA, U.S. Department of Commerce, using U.S. Census Bureau Current
Population Survey Supplements

Of the universe of Internet users, 10.0 percent of Internet users access the Internet
at a public library. This proportion remained virtually constant between August 2000
and September 2001. Over one-half of the population that uses the Internet at a public
library is under age 25. Additionally, 14.0 percent of Internet users do not use the
Internet at home, school, or work.

Internet use at public libraries varies by race and income: only 8.6 percent of
Whites that use the Internet use the public library as an access point, while the
comparable figures for Blacks and Hispanics are 18.7 percent and 13.8 percent,
respectively. Among Asian Americans and Pacific Islanders, 11.6 percent of Internet
users accessed the Internet at public libraries.

As shown in Figure 4-6, most of the people who use the Internet at public libraries
also use the Internet at other locations. Among racial and ethnic groups, 12.7 percent
of Whites, 19.4 percent of Blacks, and 16.0 percent of Hispanics using the Internet at
libraries do not also access the Internet from home, work or school. Only 6.6 percent
of Asian American and Pacific Islanders who use the Internet at a public library do not
also use the Internet from some other location.

Figure 4-6: Public Library Internet Users, by Race and Sources of Other Access as a Percent of Internet Users that Use Internet Facilities at Public Libraries

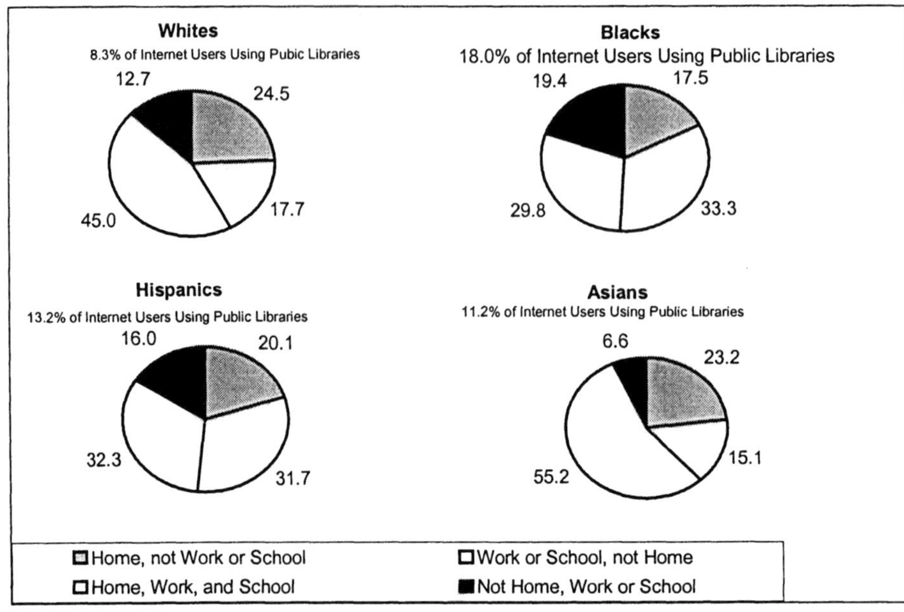

Source: NTIA and ESA, U.S. Department of Commerce, using U.S. Census Bureau Current Population Survey Supplements

Internet access at public libraries is more often used by those with lower incomes than those with higher incomes. Just over 20 percent of Internet users with household family incomes of less than $15,000 a year use public libraries, and 6.1 percent of Internet users in this income category do not use the Internet at home, work, or school. As household income rises, not only does the proportion of public library Internet users decline, but also the percentage of Internet users without alternative access points also declines.

Figure 4-7: Public Library Internet Users by Income and Location of Other Access as a Percent of Internet Users

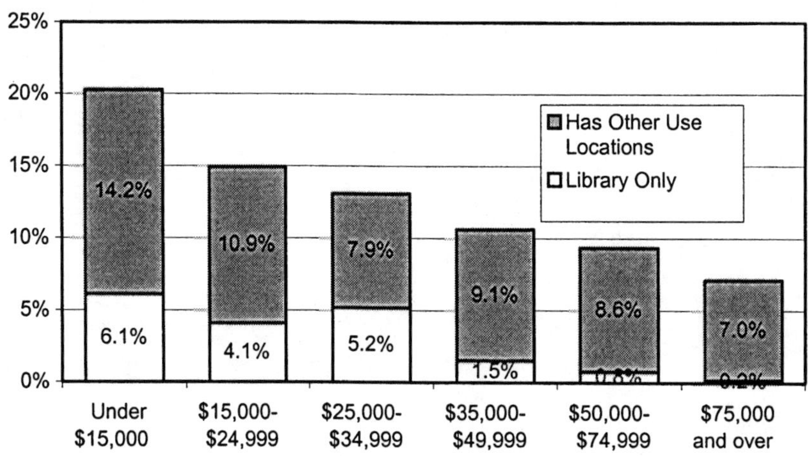

Source: NTIA and ESA, U.S. Department of Commerce, using U.S. Census Bureau Current Population Survey Supplements

THE DIGITAL GENERATION: HOW YOUNG PEOPLE HAVE EMBRACED COMPUTERS AND THE INTERNET

Children and young adults have embraced new information technologies in large numbers. More than any other age group, these younger age groups use computers and the Internet widely for many of their daily activities.

This chapter explores the increasingly large number of children and young adults who have computers and online access, where they get access outside the home, and how they use the Internet. We focus on children in lower elementary school (ages 5-9), later elementary and junior high school (ages 10-13), and high school (ages 14-17), as well as young adults (ages 18-24). This year's survey also asked parents about concerns about exposing children to online content, and whether that has affected their decisions to go online or to maintain Internet access.

COMPUTER AND INTERNET USE

As noted in Chapter 2, children and young adults under 25 are significant users of new information technologies. By the age of 10, young people are more likely to use the Internet than adults at any age beyond 25. The high rate of use among children and young adults is reflected in higher rates of Internet connectivity within family households with children, as well as in high use rates among these age groups both at home and outside the home.

Family households with children under age 18 are far more likely to have computers than families without children: 70.1 percent, compared to 58.8 percent.

They are also more likely to have Internet subscriptions: 62.2 percent versus 53.2 percent. The presence of children is also associated with modestly higher rates of broadband connectivity through DSL or cable modem: 11.9 percent for families with children, compared to 9.5 percent for those without children (Figure 5-1).

Figure 5-1: Access Among Families with and without Children, 2001 as a Percentage of U.S. Households

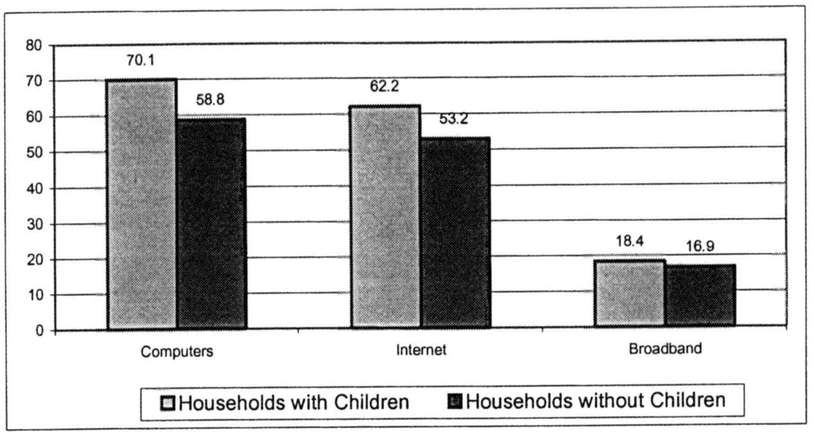

Source: NTIA and ESA, U.S. Department of Commerce, using U.S. Census Bureau Current Population Survey Supplements

Individual computer and Internet use among all groups of children and young adults has also soared in the last few years. With regard to computer use, 89.5 percent of all school-aged children (between the ages of 5-17) use computers. Within the same age range, 58.5 percent use the Internet. Internet use is particularly high for teens and pre-teens.[23] More than three-quarters (75.6 percent) of 14-17 year olds and 65.4 percent of 10-13 year olds use the Internet at some location, up from 51.2 and 39.2 percent in 1998 (Figure 5-2).

Among 18-24 year olds, Internet use is heavily affected by whether or not they attend school or college. Among those in school or college, 85.0 percent use the Internet, compared to 51.5 percent of those who are not in school.

---

[23] Figure 5-2 compares the September 2001 survey results to December 1998 Census survey data, which provided a more complete data set on student use than the August 2000 survey taken during the summer vacation.

**Figure 5-2: Internet Use at Any Location,
1998 and 2001 as a Percent of U.S. Population**

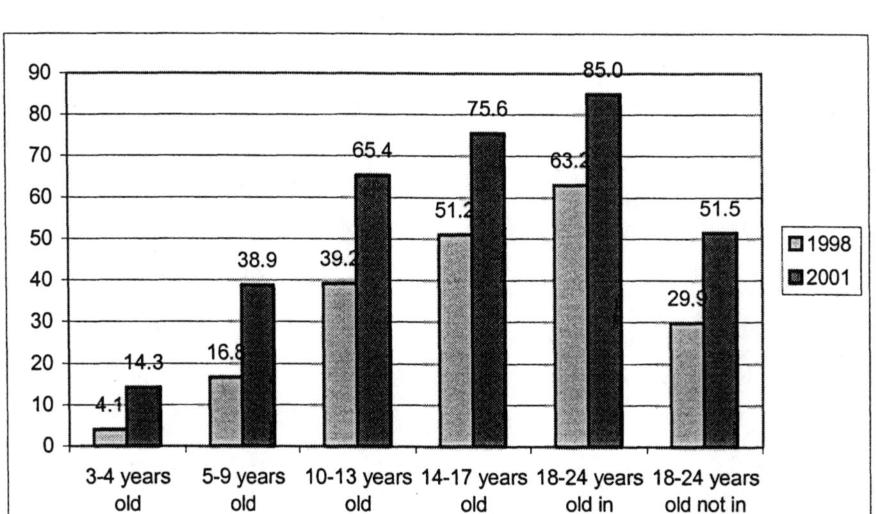

Source: NTIA and ESA, U.S. Department of Commerce, using U.S. Census Bureau Current Population Survey Supplements

In addition to much higher overall use, children and young adults are also far more likely to use the Internet outside the home than they were in previous years. In fact, "outside home" use is nearly equivalent to "at home" use for almost every age group (and exceeds "at home" use for 18-24 year olds in school or college). For example, as Figure 5-3 demonstrates, nearly equal percentages of teenagers used the Internet outside the home (60.7 percent) as at home (61.4 percent). This contrasts with 1998 levels for teenagers of 26.9 percent "outside home" use, compared to 32.9 percent at home. Similarly, in 1998, 19.2 percent of 10-13 year olds used the Internet outside the home, compared to 25.4 percent at home.

Figure 5-3: Internet Use Among Children At Home/Outside Home/Any Location, 2001 as a Percent of U.S. Population

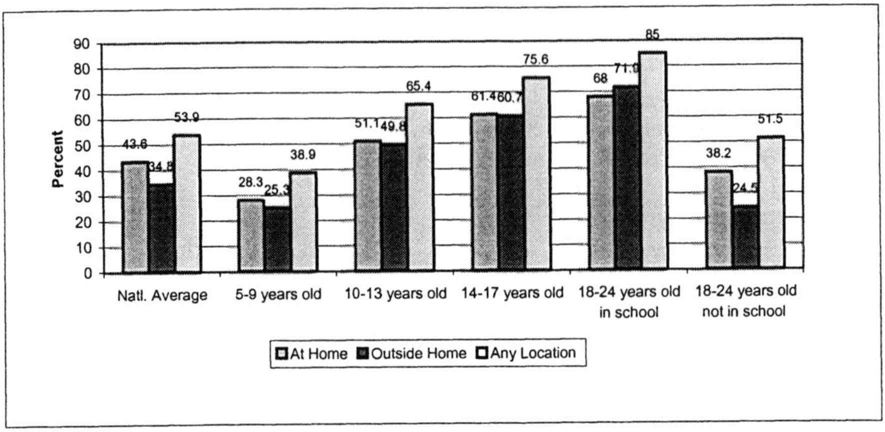

Source: NTIA and ESA, U.S. Department of Commerce, using U.S. Census Bureau Current Population Survey Supplements

THE IMPACT OF SCHOOLS ON INTERNET AND COMPUTER USE

Most "outside home" use is at schools, where children and young adults use computers and the Internet at high levels. As shown in Figure 5-4, young people are using computers at high levels, even in elementary school. For example, almost every young adult (95.9 percent) between ages 18 and 24, who attends school or college, uses a computer: 86.1 percent in school (20.8 percent only at school and 65.3 percent both at home and school), and 74.5 percent at home (9.2 percent only at home and 66.3 percent both at home and school). Even among 5 to 9 year olds, a large portion (84.3 percent) are using computers at home, at school, or both.

Figure 5-4: Computer Use by Age and Location, 2001[24]

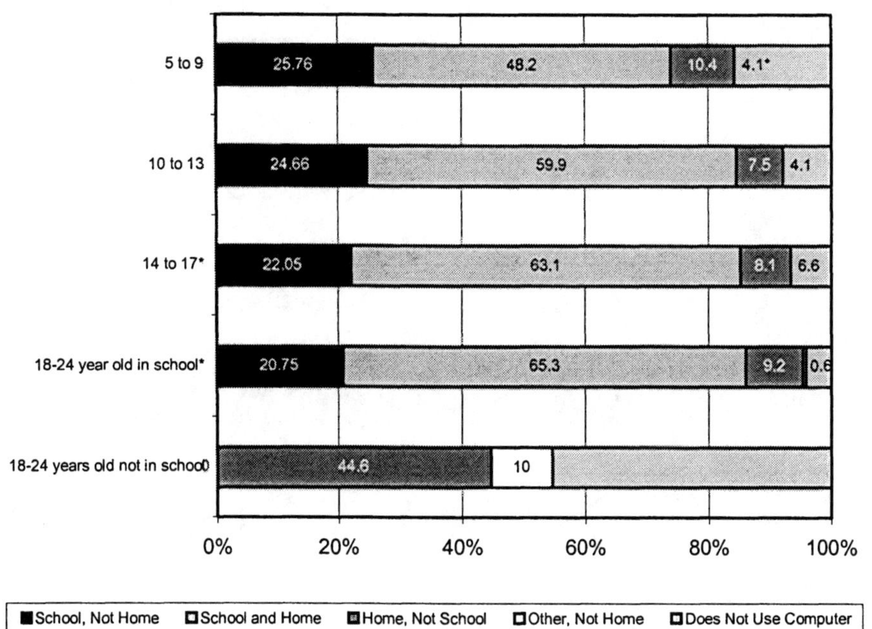

Source: NTIA and ESA, U.S. Department of Commerce, using U.S. Census Bureau Current Population Survey Supplements

Figure 5-5 also indicates the wide use of the Internet by young people both at home and at school, although Internet use is not yet at the same high levels as computer use. For example, more than three-quarters of 14-17 year olds use the Internet at home, at school, or both: 55.4 percent use the Internet at school (42.8 percent both at home and school, and 12.6 percent only at school), while 61.4 percent use it at home (42.8 percent both at home and school, and 18.6 percent only at home). Even three out of eight 5-9 year olds (or 37.6 percent) use the Internet at home and/or school.

---

[24] The percentages in the two oldest categories do not add to 100% because 0.6% of the individuals in school between the ages of 18 and 24 use a computer at work, but not at home or school and 0.1% of those between 14 and 17 use a computer at work, but not at home or school.

Figure 5-5: Internet Use by Age and Location, 2001

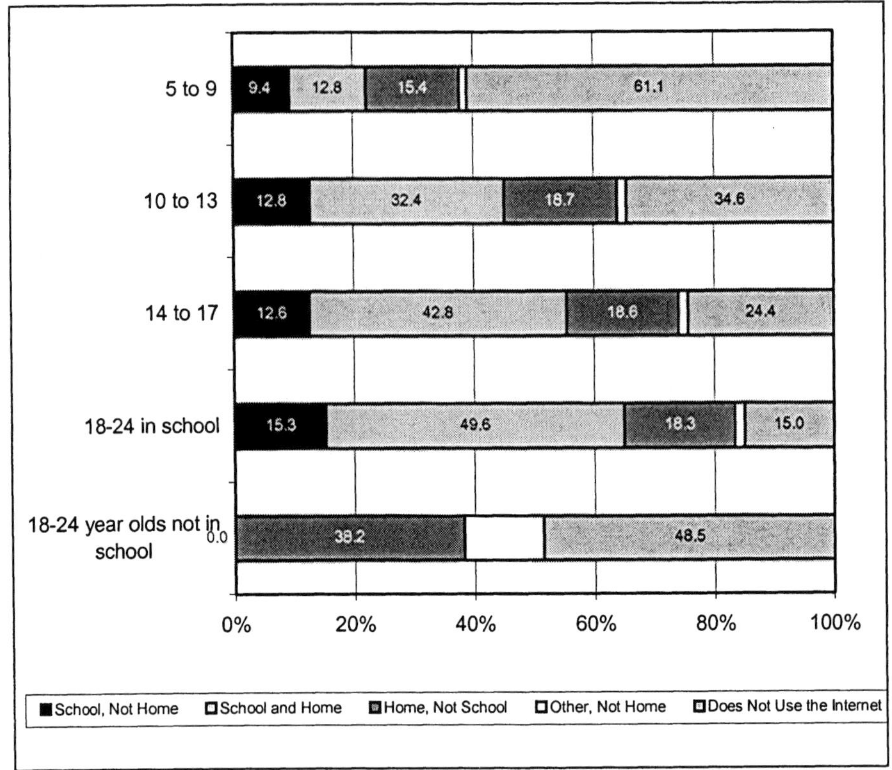

Source: NTIA and ESA, U.S. Department of Commerce, using U.S. Census Bureau Current Population Survey Supplements

Figures 5-6, 5-7, and 5-8 show the significance of having computers at school in bringing technology to children of various backgrounds.[25] Figure 5-6 shows that 80.7 percent of children (ages 10-17) in the lowest income category use computers at school, little different from the 88.7 percent of children at the highest income level. School helps to equalize the disparity that would otherwise exist in computer and Internet use among the various household income categories. In the lowest income category, 33.1 percent of children use computers at home, in contrast to 91.7 percent of children in the highest income category. The gap in computer use narrows,

---

[25] Figures 5-6 through 5-11 refer specifically to 10 to 17 year-olds. Similar patterns hold within the two component groups, 10 to 13 and 14 to 17, and for the two age groups not shown here, 5 to 9 and 18 to 24 in school. See Tables 5-1 and 5-2 for details.

however, from almost 60 points between the highest and lowest income children's use at home to a 12 point gap in computer use when home and school are combined.

Figure 5-6: Computer Use Among 10 to 17 Year-Olds By Income and Location, 2001

Thousands

Income	School, Not Home	School and Home	Home, Not School	Does Not Use a Computer
Over $75,000	5.9	82.8	8.9	2.4
$50,000-$74,999	12.0	75.0	8.8	4.3
$35,000-$49,999	20.3	67.7	6.7	5.2
$25,000-$34,999	31.8	51.8	7.4	9.0
$15,000-$24,999	42.6	39.1	5.7	12.5
Under $15,000	52.2	28.5	4.6	14.8

0%   20%   40%   60%   80%   100%

■ School, Not Home   □ School and Home   ▤ Home, Not School   □ Does Not Use a Computer

Source: NTIA and ESA, U.S. Department of Commerce, using U.S. Census Bureau Current Population Survey Supplements

Similarly, as shown in Figure 5-7, Hispanic and Black children – who have lower computer use rates at home -- approach computer use rates of Whites and Asian Americans largely due to their computer use in school. A far higher percentage of Hispanic (38.9 percent) and Black (44.7 percent) children rely solely on schools to use computers than do Asian and Pacific Islanders (11.1 percent) and White children (15.1 percent). Because of the availability of school computers, overall computer use rates among children of different racial and ethnic backgrounds is comparable: 84.2 percent for, 88.8 percent for Black children, 94 percent for Asian and Pacific Islander children, and 95.4 percent for White children.

Finally, Figure 5-8 shows that overall computer use rates for children of single parents – who have lower use rates at home – approaches those of children from two parent families due to computer use at school. More than twice as many children from single-parent families use computers only at schools as do children in two-parent families: 40.7 percent of children in female-headed households, 32.0 percent in male-headed households, and 16.6 percent in households with two parents.[26] Because of school use, children from different family types have comparable overall computer use rates: 88.8 percent for children in female-headed households, 90.7 percent for children in male-headed households, and 94.4 percent of children in dual-parent households.

**Figure 5-7: Computer Use Among 10 to 17 Year-Olds
By Race/Ethnicity and Location, 2001**

Source: NTIA and ESA, U.S. Department of Commerce, using U.S. Census Bureau Current Population Survey Supplements

---

[26] Rather than specify "mother" and "father," non-two parent households headed by a female or male could also include an aunt, uncle, grandparent, or non-relative such as a foster parent.

Figure 5-8: Computer Use Among 10 to 17 Year-Olds
By Household Type and Location, 2001

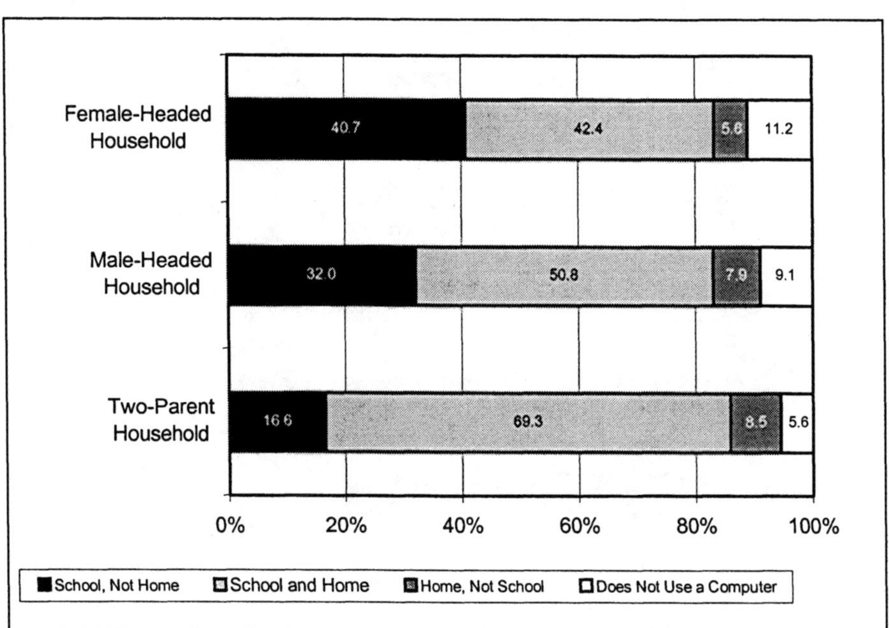

Source: NTIA and ESA, U.S. Department of Commerce, using U.S. Census Bureau Current Population Survey Supplements

Schools also provide an important resource for Internet use for all children, regardless of their background. The levels of school-only Internet use, however, are not as high as the levels of school-only computer use. As a result, the availability of the Internet at schools does not compensate for disparities in home use to the same degree as computer use in schools.

As shown in Figures 5-9, 5-10, and 5-11, substantial differences in overall Internet use remain between children of different backgrounds. Figure 5-9 demonstrates that nearly four times as many children (ages 10-17) go online only at school when they live in a household in the lowest income category (20.8 percent) than at the highest income level (5.0 percent). However, overall school use still varies widely: 34.3 percent for children in the lowest income category, compared to 62.7 percent for children who live in the highest income households. Additionally, home Internet use is much higher for those who live in high income households: 82.5 percent for children in families earning $75,000 and higher, compared to 21.4 percent for children in families earning $15,000 and below). For these reasons, overall Internet use among children has a wider differential by income than computer use. Children in families at the lowest income level have an overall Internet use rate about half that of children at the highest income level: 45.7 percent, compared to 87.5 percent.

Figure 5-9: Internet Use Among 10 to 17 Year-Olds by Income and Location, 2001

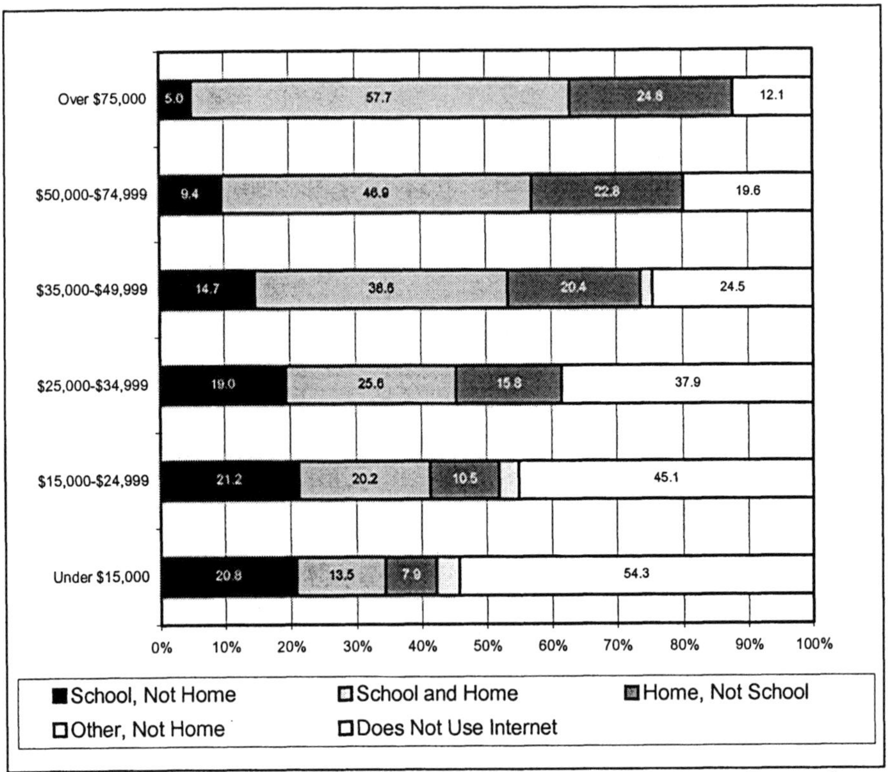

Source: NTIA and ESA, U.S. Department of Commerce, using U.S. Census Bureau Current Population Survey Supplements

Figure 5-10 demonstrates that there are also significant differences in online use among children of different races and ethnicities. School-only and home use rates are relatively lower for Hispanic and Black children, resulting in overall use rates of 47.8 and 52.3 percent, respectively. Asian American and Pacific Islander and White children, by contrast, are far more likely to use the Internet either at home only, or at home and school, resulting in higher overall Internet use levels of 79.4 and 79.7 percent, respectively.

Figure 5-10: Internet Use Among 10 to 17
Year-Olds by Race/Ethnicity and Location, 2001

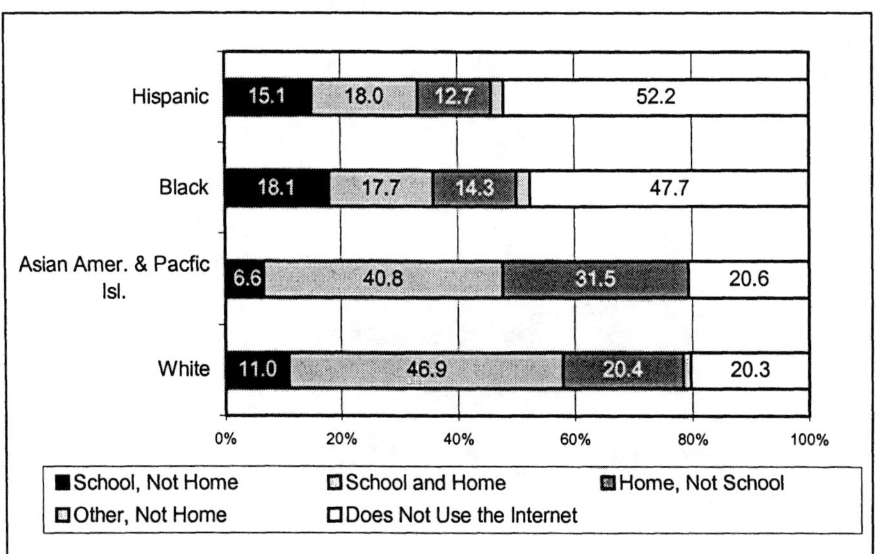

Source: NTIA and ESA, U.S. Department of Commerce, using U.S. Census Bureau Current Population Survey Supplements

Finally, Figure 5-11 shows similar patterns for children from households of different family types. Children in single-parent families are less likely to use the Internet at home (36.5 percent in female-headed households and 45.1 percent in male-headed households) than are children in two-parent families (64.2 percent). Because Internet use at school does not compensate for this difference, overall Internet use rates remain higher for children in two-parent families.

While the vast majority of children and young adults uses the Internet either at home or school, there are some who use the Internet at other locations outside the home. This is captured in the "other only" category in Figures 5-9, 5-10, and 5-11. Approximately 12 percent of 10 to17 year olds use the Internet at the library and a similar percentage use the Internet at a friend's house. (one-third of this group overlaps—*i.e.*, they use the Internet at both the library and a friend's house). However, as shown in the figures above, only a very small percentage of Internet users in this age group rely solely on Internet access outside of home and school—2.1 percent— although this does vary by family income, race/ethnicity, and household type, as discussed in Chapter 2.

Using the Internet from a location other than home or school also varies by whether the student has Internet access at home. For example, 16.6 percent of Internet users in the 10-17 age bracket use the Internet at a public library. This percentage, however, rises to 29.3 percent among kids who use the Internet at school, but not at home. And although there are large differences in public library use among the various segments of this group (see Figure 5-12), overall public library use remains high for students who use the Internet at school, but not at home.

Figure 5-11: Internet Use Among 10 to 17 Year-Olds by Household Type, 2001

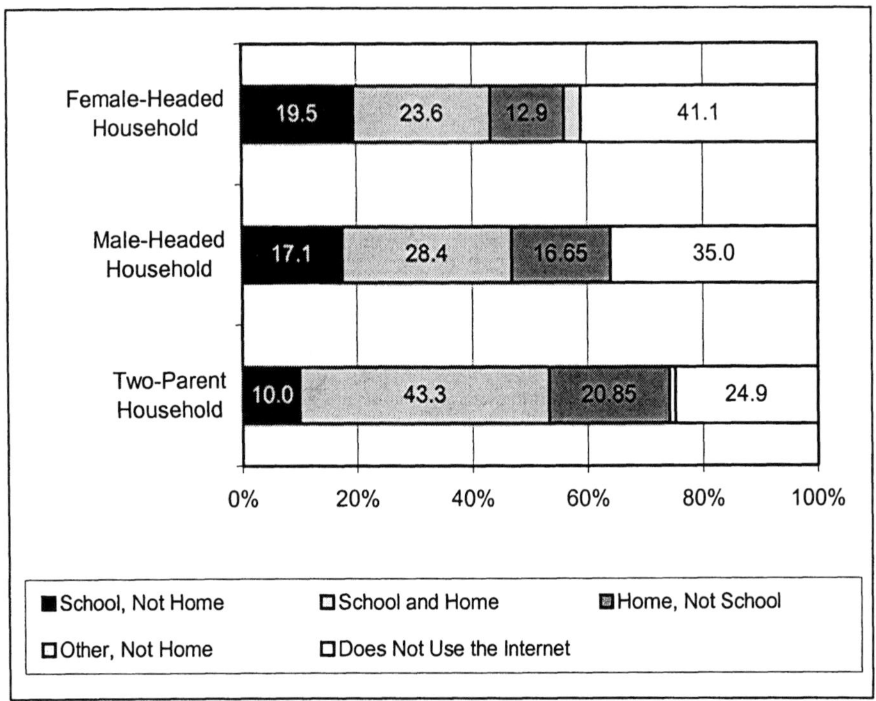

Source: NTIA and ESA, U.S. Department of Commerce, using U.S. Census Bureau Current Population Survey Supplements

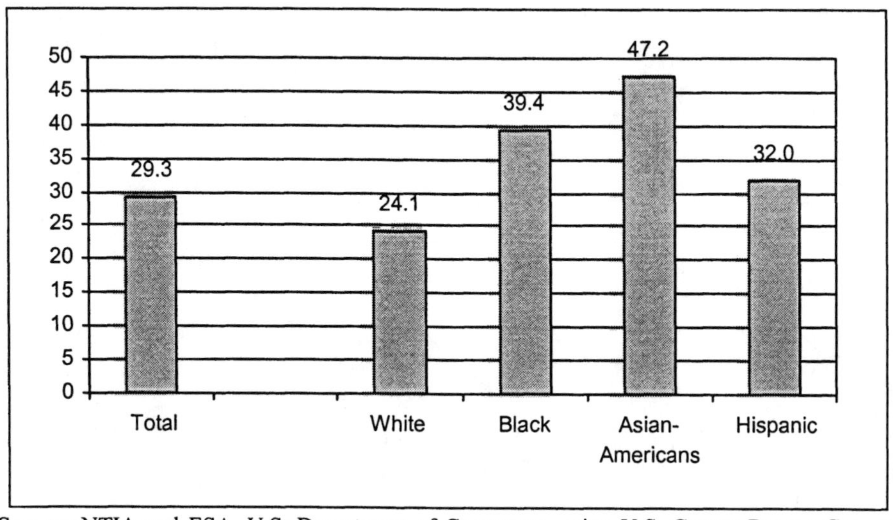

Figure 5-12: Internet Use at Public Libraries by Students Who Use the Internet at School, But Not at Home, Ages 10 to 17, 2001

Source: NTIA and ESA, U.S. Department of Commerce, using U.S. Census Bureau Current Population Survey Supplements

HOW YOUNG PEOPLE ARE USING THE INTERNET

Children and young adults have embraced the Internet in conducting their daily activities, and therefore use the Internet in ways that differ from older adults. While older adults tend to use the Internet to check for news, sports, weather, or research products and services, children and young adults are more likely to use the Internet to complete school assignments or play games. And while very high percentages of all age groups – adults and children alike – use e-mail, older children and young adults are doing so at much higher levels.

As shown in Figure 5-13, children and young adults are most likely to use the Internet for school work. More than half of all children over age 10, and three-quarters of all young adults (18 to 24 year olds) in school, use the Internet for this purpose. Nearly one-fifth of all elementary school students are also using the Internet for school work.

Children and young adults also use the Internet for communication and entertainment. E-mail is a close second to school work among teenagers and young adults. A very high percentage of all teenagers (62.1 percent) and young adults in school (75.0 percent) use e-mail, compared to 45.2 percent of the overall U.S.

population. These two age groups also go online in higher percentages than other age groups to engage in chat rooms and to listen to the radio or watch TV or movies.

Generally, as children grow older, they use the Internet for more types of activities. The one exception is playing games, which peaks among 14-17 year olds. While Internet use is generally lower among 5-9 year olds, 25 percent of this age group uses the Internet to play games.

Figure 5-13: Major Activities Among Children and Young Adults, 2001 As a Percentage of U.S. Population under 25 years old

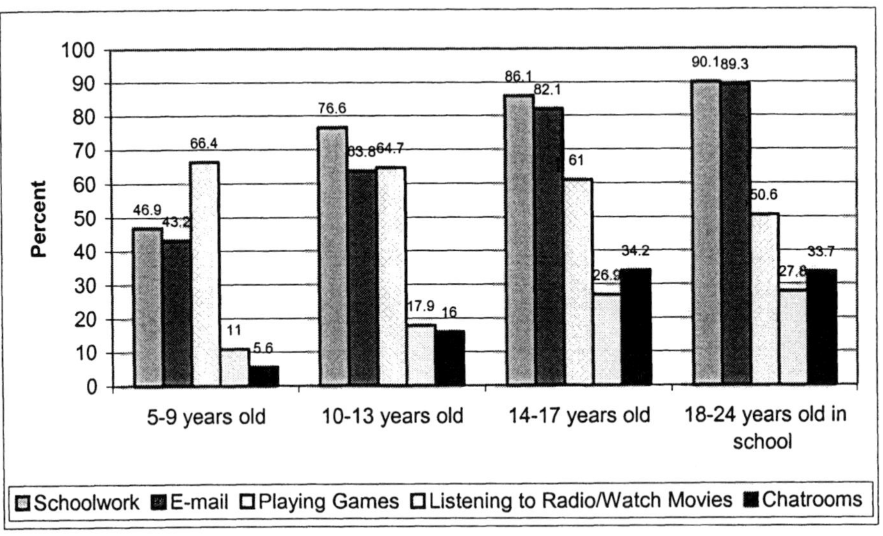

Source: NTIA and ESA, U.S. Department of Commerce, using U.S. Census Bureau Current Population Survey Supplements

These patterns show that the Internet has become integrated into children's daily routines, which involve school, entertainment, communication, and play. As children get older, they become far more likely to use the Internet to engage in such activities. As a result, teenagers and young adults in school are now among the highest Internet users.

CONCERNS ABOUT CHILDREN'S ONLINE USE

With the Internet becoming an increasingly common daily activity for children, there has been a heightened interest regarding the possible exposure of children to unsafe or inappropriate content online. Despite such concerns, it is clear that children are still using the Internet in increasingly high numbers. As discussed below, it is also apparent that these concerns are not a significant reason underlying a household's decision to forego or to discontinue Internet access. Nevertheless, because these concerns have been raised, the September 2001 survey asked for the first time whether parents were more concerned about exposure of children to material on the Internet or to material on television.[27]

On a nationwide basis, a majority of respondents (68.3 percent) said that they were more concerned about their children's exposure to material over the Internet. A lower percentage said they felt equally concerned about the propriety of Internet and television content (26.1 percent), and a small fraction (5.6 percent) said they felt less concerned about the Internet than television.

The concern about exposing children to inappropriate online content does not, however, result in lower levels of Internet use at home. More people who expressed concern about the Internet than television had Internet subscriptions at home (51.8 percent), than those who were more concerned about television (44.8 percent) or felt equally about the Internet and television (46.9 percent)

Additionally, even though more respondents stated concern about the Internet than television, this concern was seldom a factor when households opted to discontinue an Internet subscription or made the decision not to subscribe. When households that had discontinued Internet access were asked why, "concerns about how children use it" was one of the least cited factors (2.5 percent nationwide, compared to "too expensive" at 21.8 percent or "don't want it" at 20.0 percent). Married couples with children under 18 were more likely, however, to list concerns about children as their reason for discontinuing access (6.6 percent), as were male-headed households (5.3 percent) and female-headed households (4.8 percent).

Similarly, only 1 percent of households nationwide that never had an Internet subscription cited "concerns about how children use it" as a reason (compared to 53.6 percent that cited "don't want it" and 23.8 percent that cited "too expensive"). Again, married couples with children under 18 were slightly more likely to cite this reason (5.3 percent), as were single mothers (1.9 percent) and single fathers (1.4 percent), although still at very low levels.

In sum, while survey respondents generally expressed more concern about the effect of the Internet than television on children, this concern does not appear to have prompted families to discontinue or reject Internet access at home compared to other factors.

---

[27] While the survey captured which medium caused parents greater concern, it did not capture the level of concern. The respondent might state that he or she felt "more concerned" about the Internet, but the survey does not measure whether the concern is slight or extreme.

Table 5-1: Has Computer at Home and Uses Internet at Home, by Children 3-17 Years Old, 2001

	Total 3-17 Years Old	Home Computer	Home Internet Use	Outside Home Internet Use
	Number	Percent	Percent	Percent
Total	60,881	70.7	41.2	38.9
AGE				
3-4 years	7,868	61.7	11.5	5.4
5-9 years	20,096	68.0	28.3	25.3
10-13 years	16,895	88.5	51.1	49.8
14-17 years	16,022	75.7	61.4	60.7
GENDER				
Male	31,183	70.3	41.1	38.7
Female	29,699	71.1	41.2	39.0
RACE/HISPANIC ORIGIN				
White non-Hispanic	38,170	82.7	50.2	44.5
Black	9,477	45.8	24.7	31.8
Asian Pacific Islander	2,591	81.3	51.6	37.3
Hispanic (of any race)	9,923	46.6	20.1	24.5
HOUSEHOLD TYPE				
Married-couple household	42,835	79.1	46.6	40.0
Male householder	3,093	57.2	33.0	37.8
Female householder	14,166	49.0	26.8	35.9
Nonfamily household	669	55.0	31.7	32.7
FAMILY INCOME				
Under $15,000	7,323	33.3	14.3	25.9
15,000-24,999	6,108	48.0	21.4	31.5
25,000-34,999	6,765	59.7	28.9	33.6
35,000-49,999	8,632	75.7	42.4	41.7
50,000-74,999	10,840	86.9	52.1	44.0
75,000+	13,604	94.9	63.4	48.3
Not reported	7,596	62.6	37.1	34.4

Source: NTIA and ESA, U.S. Department of Commerce, using U.S. Census Bureau Current Population Survey Supplements

Table 5-2: Has Computer at Home and Uses Internet at Home by Young Adults 18-24 Years Old, Attending School or College, 2001

	Total 18-24 Years Old	Home Computer	Home Internet Use	Outside Home Internet Use
	Number	Percent	Percent	Percent
In School or College	11,034	80.7	68.0	71.9
Not in School or College	16,103	52.4	24.0	13.3
GENDER				
Male	5,195	81.9	69.4	73.7
Female	5,833	89.1	66.8	70.3
RACE/HISPANIC ORIGIN				
White non-Hispanic	7,499	86.5	74.3	76.2
Black	1,450	58.9	47.0	59.7
Asian Pacific Islander	730	89.6	77.5	72.5
Hispanic (of any race)	1,288	66.8	49.7	61.1
HOUSEHOLD TYPE				
Married-couple household	3,346	88.3	73.8	69.3
Male householder	264	66.7	53.8	69.3
Female householder	1,059	60.0	46.5	58.7
Non-family household	1,854	78.6	68.6	81.4
FAMILY INCOME				
Under $15,000	1,550	69.2	56.1	73.9
15,000-24,999	902	68.7	53.8	65.2
25,000-34,999	1,004	68.4	56.1	73.0
35,000-49,999	1,173	81.8	37.5	67.8
50,000-74,999	1,766	87.7	34.5	74.0
75,000+	3,147	93.8	83.0	75.6
Not reported	1,493	71.2	62.8	64.7

Source: NTIA and ESA, U.S. Department of Commerce, using U.S. Census Bureau Current Population Survey Supplements

While school is the primary location where children use computers and the Internet outside the home, for adults that location is the workplace, which is discussed in the next chapter.

Chapter 6

THE DIGITAL WORKPLACE

INTRODUCTION

The workplace provides an important venue for many adults to use computers and the Internet. As of September 2001, about 65 million of the 115 million adults who were employed and age 25 and over use a computer at work. About 48 million of these adults (the vast majority of the 53 million in this group who use the Internet outside the home) connect to the Internet and/or use e-mail at work.[28]

In the last four years, the percentage of adults who use computers at work rose modestly while the percentage using the Internet and/or e-mail at work grew appreciably, especially in the thirteen months between August 2000 and September 2001.[29] During this thirteen-month period, use of the Internet at work among employed adults aged 25 and over increased from 26.1 percent to 41.7 percent.

---

[28] In contrast, only about 4 million of the 62 million adults who are age 25 and over and not employed used the Internet outside the home.

[29] In October 1997, questions about computer use at work covered mainframes, minis and personal computers, while in September 2001 questions focused on desktop and laptop computers. The wording of questions about Internet use at work in 1997, 1998, 2000 and 2001 differed somewhat as well. See Figure 1-1.

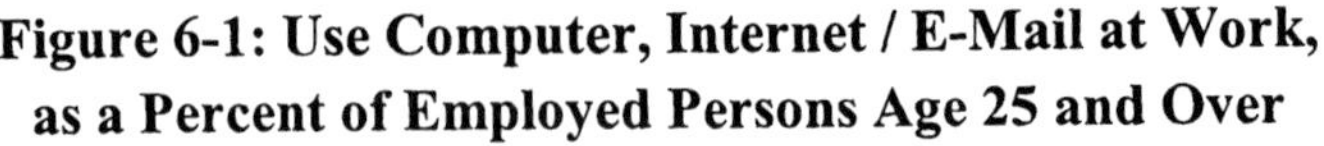

**Figure 6-1: Use Computer, Internet / E-Mail at Work,
as a Percent of Employed Persons Age 25 and Over**

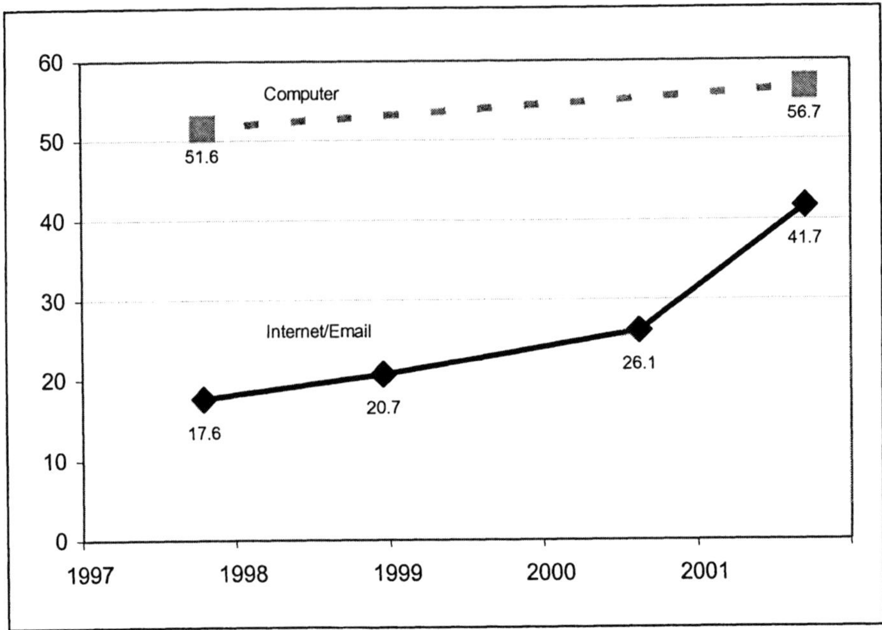

Source: NTIA and ESA, U.S. Department of Commerce, using U.S. Census Bureau Current Population Survey Supplements

COMPUTER USE AT WORK BY OCCUPATION

In general, use of a computer at work correlates with occupations in which workers have higher educational attainment and, to a lesser extent, with gender.

The proportion of people using a computer at work was 80.5 percent for people in managerial and professional specialty occupations and was 70.5 percent for people in technical, sales, and administrative support occupations. The median educational attainment in these fields is a college degree or some college enrollments. About three-quarters of employed women work in these two occupations in contrast with just over one-half of men.

Table 6-1: Employed Persons Age 25 & Over, by Occupation

	Employed (000s)	Median Education	Percent women	Use a computer at main job	
				000s	Percent
Total	115,065	SC	46.3	65,190	56.7
Managerial and professional specialty	39,412	CD	50.2	31,723	80.5
Technical, sales, and administrative support	31,482	SC	62.9	22,205	70.5
Precision production, craft, and repair	13,083	HS	8.4	4,152	31.7
Service	13,678	HS	61.6	3,478	25.4
Operators, fabricators, and laborers	14,504	HS	24.3	3,006	20.7
Farming, forestry, and fishing	2,905	HS	20.3	625	21.5
CD – college degree, SC – some college but no degree, HS – high school diploma or GED					

Source: NTIA and ESA, U.S. Department of Commerce, using U.S. Census Bureau Current Population Survey Supplements

At the other end of the spectrum, only about one in five persons used a computer at work in the occupation categories for operators, fabricators, and laborers as well as for farming, forestry, and fishing. The median educational attainment in these fields is a high school diploma. Women account for less than ten percent of those employed in these occupations.

COMPUTER USE AT WORK BY GENDER AND AGE

Because of the occupational differences, women were more likely to use a computer at their main job (62.9 percent to 51.3 percent). This difference persisted across all ages. For both men and women, the percentage using a computer at work remained fairly constant across all ages until they reached their mid- to late 50s, at which point computer use at work for both genders declined steadily.

**Figure 6-2: Use of a Computer at Work by Gender and Age
Percent of Employed Persons, 2001**

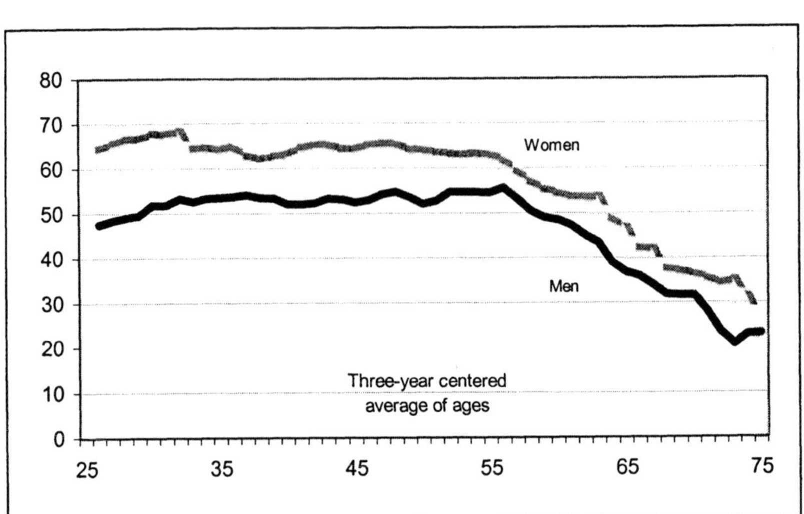

Source: NTIA and ESA, U.S. Department of Commerce, using U.S. Census Bureau Current
Population Survey Supplements

TYPES OF COMPUTER USES AT WORK

Workplace use of computers involves a number of tasks, led by connecting to the
Internet, word processing, and spreadsheets and databases. Calendar and scheduling,
graphics and design, and programming are less commonly used applications.

Not surprisingly, the ranking of computer activities at work by occupation tends to
follow the order for general use of a computer at work. Workers in managerial and
professional specialties, as well as technical, sales, and administrative support, are the
most active users of the Internet and e-mail, word processing, spreadsheets and
databases, and calendar and scheduling.

Figure 6-3: Computer Activities at Work, as a Percent of Employed Persons Age 25 and Over, 2001

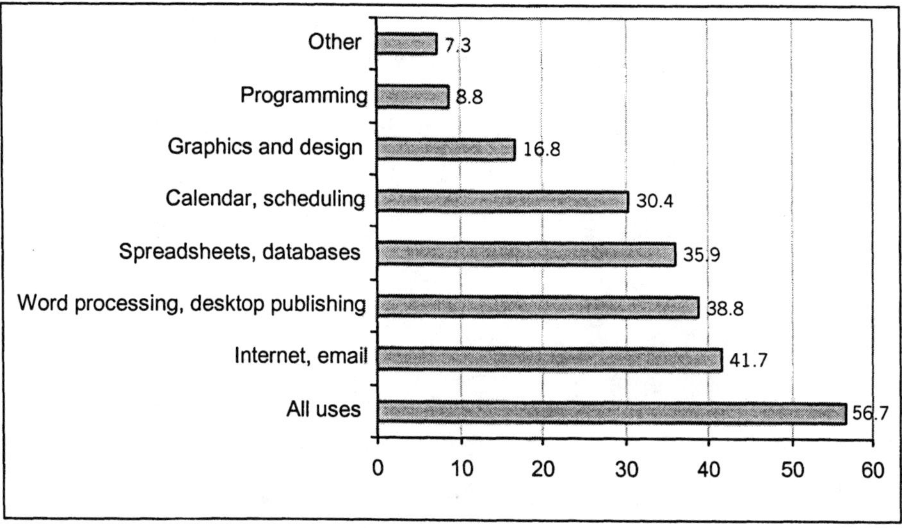

Source: NTIA and ESA, U.S. Department of Commerce, using U.S. Census Bureau Current Population Survey Supplements

Table 6-2: Top Four Computer Uses by Occupation, Percent of Employed Persons 25 & Over

	Internet, e-mail	Word processing, desktop publishing	Spread-sheets, databases	Calendar, scheduling
Total	41.7	38.8	35.9	30.4
Managerial and professional specialty	66.8	63.2	56.6	48.8
Technical, sales, and administrative support	49.2	45.5	43.1	34.7
Service	13.9	14.3	11.8	12.3
Precision production, craft, and repair	19.0	14.8	16.6	14.6
Operators, fabricators, and laborers	9.2	7.6	8.7	7.0
Farming, forestry, and fishing	14.6	13.0	13.2	9.2

Source: NTIA and ESA, U.S. Department of Commerce, using U.S. Census Bureau Current Population Survey Supplements

INTERNET USE AT WORK

The proportion of employed persons age 25 and/ over who use the Internet and/or e-mail at work increased from 26.1 percent in August 2000 to 41.7 percent in September 2001, a vigorous 54 percent annual rate of growth.

As with computer use, employed persons age 25 and over who use the Internet at work were not evenly distributed by age or gender. Women are more likely than men to use the Internet/e-mail at work: 44.4 percent compared with 39.3 percent. This margin in favor of women is about half of the margin for computer use.

Also similar to computer use, the proportion of men and women who use the Internet at work remains reasonably steady between the ages of 25 and 55, when Internet use at work dropped off. The margin in favor of women persists until the mid-50s, at which point it essentially disappears.

**Figure 6-4: Use Internet / E-mail at Work by Gender and Age,
as a Percent of Employed Persons, 2001**

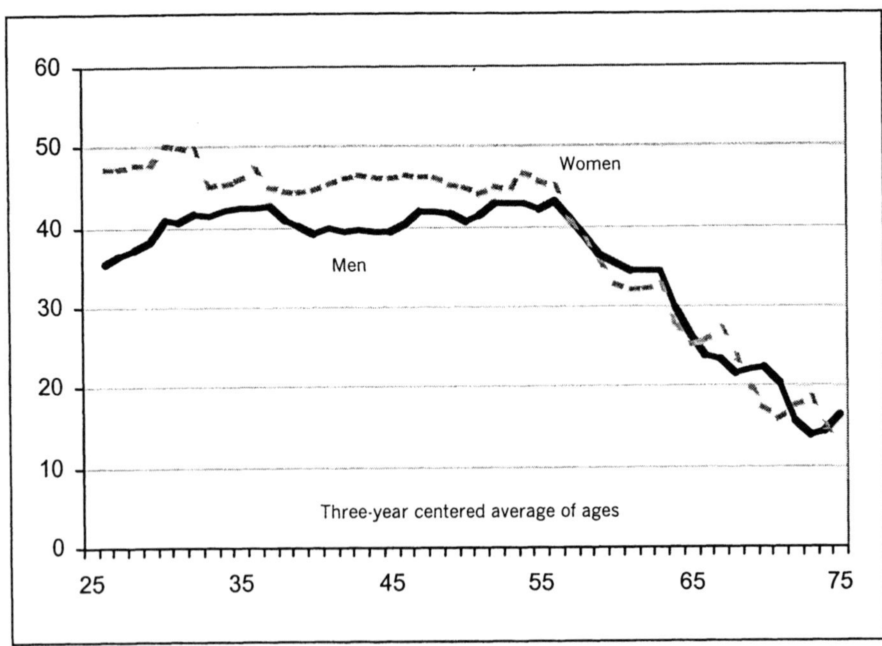

Source: NTIA and ESA, U.S. Department of Commerce, using U.S. Census Bureau Current Population Survey Supplements

Occupations already more likely to be using the Internet at work tended to experience the largest gains in Internet/e-mail use between 2000 and 2001 on a percentage point basis. In terms of growth rates, however, farming, forestry, and fishing and service occupations posted the largest advances.

Figure 6-5: Internet / E-mail Use at Work by Occupation, as a Percent of Employed Persons Age 25 and Over, 2001

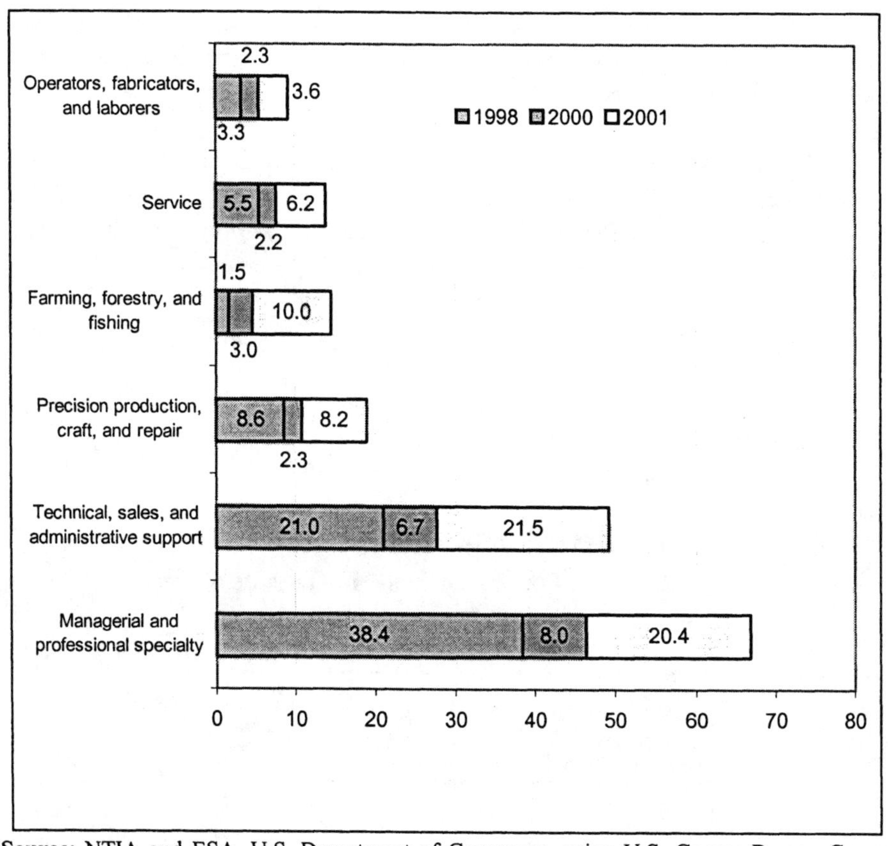

Source: NTIA and ESA, U.S. Department of Commerce, using U.S. Census Bureau Current Population Survey Supplements

Even with recent gains, striking differences in Internet use at work by occupation remain, particularly in male-dominated fields. While information technology undoubtedly can play a role in many fields of work, there are some occupations where it may be of little or no value or take a different form than a desktop computer connected to the Internet. In addition, further advances in the state of the art in computers in terms of reliability, portability, and ease of use may be necessary before they are practical in occupations characterized by lower levels of educational attainment.

THE WORK – HOME CONNECTION

Approximately 24 million of the 65 million employed adults who use a computer at work also use a computer at home to do work. This underscores a critical connection between the workplace and home: exposure to a computer and the Internet in the workplace makes it substantially more likely for a computer and the Internet to be used at home.

While undoubtedly, there are cases where enthusiastic home users are responsible for introducing computers and the Internet to a workplace, the far more common direction of transmission likely is from work to home. Use at work not only acquaints someone with the utility of the technology, it also provides an opportunity to climb a sometimes frustrating learning curve in an environment with technical support. This acquired knowledge can then be taken home and shared with other members of a household.

The presence of someone who uses a computer or the Internet at work in a household is associated with substantially higher computer ownership or Internet use for that household, by a margin of about 77 percent to 35 percent.

Table 6-3: Computer Ownership and Internet Access by Presence of Work Users, Percent of U.S. Households, 2001

	Percent of U.S. Households with:	
	Computer	Internet access
All households	56.5	50.5
Does any household member use at work:		
Yes	77.9	76.8
No	35.9	34.8

Source: NTIA and ESA, U.S. Department of Commerce, using U.S. Census Bureau Current Population Survey Supplements

Table 6-4: Internet Access of Selected Households by Presence of Work Users, as a Percent of U.S. Households, 2001

		Someone in household uses Internet at work	
	Total	**Yes**	**No**
All households	50.5	76.8	34.8
Income, Under $15,000	17.7	57.2	14.8
Less than high school education	18.2	54.2	14.5
Income, $15,000 – 24,999	28.3	52.2	23.8
Black	30.9	59.1	20.7
Hispanic	32.0	63.1	22.1
Age 55 and over	33.9	71.6	25.5
Other than income, characteristics are for reference person of household			

Source: NTIA and ESA, U.S. Department of Commerce, using U.S. Census Bureau Current Population Survey Supplements

The much greater likelihood of household access associated with workplace use not only occurs in the aggregate but also is evident across all age groups, income brackets, educational levels, and race/Hispanic origin. The margin is especially large in groups that lag behind the national average, reflecting the small proportion of these households that contain someone who uses the Internet at work.

These results point to the need for caution in interpreting the direct effect of single variables such as income on Internet use at home. When we consider only households in which someone is using the Internet at work, at least half of those households have Internet at home even in the lowest income categories or in households in which no one completed high school. Among households with less than $15,000 in income, the few households with someone using the Internet at work are four times as likely to have the Internet at home as those without such a person. The steepness of the typical gradient for income or education alone is thus misleading because it represents a weighted average of households that differ in a fundamental way.

Figure 6-6: Household Internet Access by Family Income, as a Percent of U.S. Households, 2001

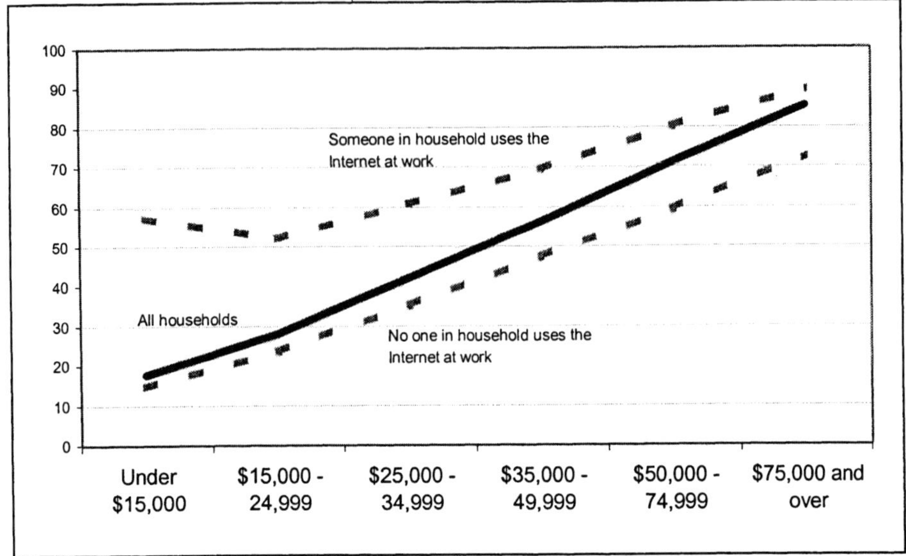

Source: NTIA and ESA, U.S. Department of Commerce, using U.S. Census Bureau Current Population Survey Supplements

Figure 6-7: Household Internet Access by Education, as a Percent of U.S. Households, 2001

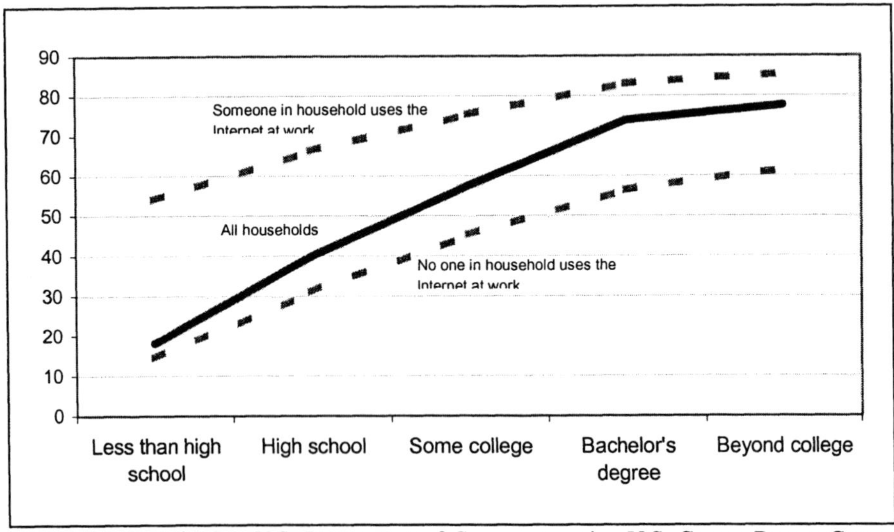

Source: NTIA and ESA, U.S. Department of Commerce, using U.S. Census Bureau Current Population Survey Supplements

Chapter 7

COMPUTER AND INTERNET USE AMONG PEOPLE WITH DISABILITIES

As demonstrated in earlier sections, computer and Internet use is becoming increasingly commonplace in homes, schools, and on the job. People of all ages, races, and ethnicities are moving more and more of their activities online. Having access and the ability to use these tools is especially important to members of our community who have difficulties due to physical or mental constraints. The tremendous communications capabilities of the Internet could provide an important tool to help people with disabilities to overcome certain of the challenges they face. However, the data show that people with disabilities are less likely than the population as a whole to use computers or the Internet.

PEOPLE WITH DISABILITIES

The September 2001 supplement marks the first time that questions about specific types of disability have been included in the set of computer and Internet use questions on the Current Population Survey (CPS).[30] These questions do not attempt to quantify

---

[30] The previous report, *Falling Through the Net: Toward Digital Inclusion*, published in October 2000, did include a section on "Internet Access and Computer Use Among People with Disabilities." The data for that section, however, came from another survey, the Survey of Income and Program Participation, which, in the fall of 1999 asked different questions to identify persons with disabilities from those used in the September 2001 CPS supplement. The CPS does allow respondents to choose "disability" as a reason for not being in the work force. However, as this section shows, most people with a disability do not fall into this category. The September supplement to the CPS through 2005 is scheduled to include questions on both computer/Internet use and on disability. Thus, future reports should be able to document changes in computer and Internet use among people with diabilities.

the number or the proportion of people in the population who have a disability. Rather, these questions were posed in order to examine how specific types of disabilities impact computer and Internet use. The questions, as asked, are shown in Box 7-1. They cover long-lasting severe vision, hearing, mobility, and manual dexterity problems, as well as a question concerning any physical or mental condition that makes it difficult to leave the house.

Box 7-1: CPS Supplement Questions Concerning Specific Types of Disabilities

---

Do you have any of the following long-lasting physical conditions:
(Asked of everyone in the household age 3 and above)

    A) Blindness or a severe vision impairment even with glasses or contact lenses?

    B) Deafness or a severe hearing impairment even with a hearing aid?

    C) A physical condition that substantially limits your ability to walk or climb stairs?

    D) A condition that makes it difficult to type on an ordinary typewriter or traditional computer keyboard?

Do you have difficulty going outside the home alone, for example, to shop or visit a doctor's office, because of a physical or mental health condition lasting six months or longer?
(Asked of everyone in the household age 15 and above)

Approximately 8.5 percent of the population has at least one of the five disabilities covered in the survey. As shown in Table 7-1, the incidence of each of the various types of disabilities rises sharply with age. For example, while only 1.3 percent of children under 15 have at least one of the disabilities examined here, almost 30 percent of the population aged 65 and older has at least one of these limitations. Because this pattern is the reverse of that followed by Internet use (which rises sharply at the younger end of the spectrum and then declines at older age levels, see Figure 2-5 in Chapter 2), it is important to consider the question of computer and Internet use by people with disabilities within relevant age categories.[31] However, the relatively few respondents who have these disabilities at the lower end of the age range and the relatively few respondents who use computers and the Internet at the upper end of the

---

[31] For example, on average only 25.4 percent of the population aged 3 and above with at least one of the first four types of disabilities (difficulty leaving home not included because it was only asked of age 15 and above) use the Internet at any location. Part of the reason this percentage is so much lower than the 53.9 percent average for the population as a whole, is that the population of people with disabilities is heavily weighted toward an older population that is less likely to use the Internet.

age range severely limit the degree of disaggregation that can be undertaken. Therefore, this analysis is limited to three broad groups: individuals under 25, 25 to 60 year-olds, and those over 60.

Under 25[32]

Less than 2 percent of the population between ages 3 and 24 reported having at least one of the disabilities considered in this report. Table 7-2 contains the only relevant data on computer and Internet use that can reliably be presented for this age group. Although "Internet Use at Home" is lower among those with disabilities, Internet use from other locations brings those with either severe vision or hearing impairments up to the level of the population in general and substantially improves the connectivity situation of individuals in the other disability categories. While a reasonable assumption would be that many of these young people have Internet access through their school, this cannot be demonstrated with this survey data because of the small number of observations in this category.

**Table 7-1: Age Distribution of Specific Disabilities
as a Percent of Population, 2001**

	3-14	15-24	25-34	35-44	45-54	55-64	65 and Over
Multiple Disabilities	0.4	0.6	1.0	2.0	3.8	6.3	15.0
Blind or Severe Vision Impairment	0.3	0.4	0.4	0.5	0.6	0.7	1.4
Deaf or Severe Hearing Impairment	0.3	0.3	0.3	0.5	0.6	0.9	2.4
Difficulty Walking	0.2	0.4	1.0	1.9	2.7	5.7	7.1
Difficulty Typing	0.1	0.3	0.4	0.6	0.6	0.8	0.9
Difficulty Leaving Home	Not Asked	0.5	0.5	0.7	0.9	1.1	2.2
None of These Disabilities	98.7	97.6	96.4	93.8	90.7	84.6	71.1

Source: NTIA and ESA, U.S. Department of Commerce, using U.S. Census Bureau Current Population Survey Supplements

---

[32] The population totals for the age groups in this section are less than for the CPS supplement in general because this section is necessarily limited to those respondents who answered the questions concerning disability.

Table 7-2: Computer and Internet Use Among 3 to 24 Year-Olds by Disability Status, 2001

	Size of Population in Category (000s)	Percent of Population (%)	Has a PC at Home (%)	Uses the Internet at Home (%)	Uses the Internet from Any Location (%)
Multiple Disabilities	436	0.6	65.0	26.8	43.6
Blind or Severe Vision Impairment	267	0.4	61.2	30.6	56.3
Deaf or Severe Hearing Impairment	198	0.3	76.4	26.6	56.5
Difficulty Walking	275	0.4	64.0	32.4	45.8
Difficulty Typing	185	0.2	63.9	35.4	48.6
None of These Disabilities	75,299	98.2	68.5	43.8	56.9
Total Answering	76,659		68.4	43.5	56.7
% not answering	12.9				

Source: NTIA and ESA, U.S. Department of Commerce, using U.S. Census Bureau Current Population Survey Supplements

25 to 60 year olds

Among individuals between the ages of 25 and 60, the incidence of their having at least one of the five disabilities considered here increases to 7.3 percent. As shown in Table 7-3 below, with the exception of those individuals with severe hearing impairment, those who have at least one of these disabilities are less likely than those without a disability to live in a home with a personal computer. And even in homes with a computer, people who have at least one of these disabilities are less likely to use the computer or the Internet.

People who have at least one of the listed disabilities are much less likely to be Internet users than those without any of these disabilities. Further, even among Internet users, the Internet activities of people with disabilities are somewhat different. As shown in Table 7-4, people with disabilities are more likely than the population in general to use the Internet to play games and search for health information.

Table 7-3: Computer and Internet Use at Home among 25 to 60 Year-Olds By Disability Status, 2001

	Size of Population in Category (000s)	Percent of Population (%)	Has a Computer at Home (%)	Of Those Who Have a PC at Home	
				Uses as the PC at Home (%)	Uses the Internet at Home (%)
Multiple Disabilities	3,111.2	2.6	45.4	67.8	56.4
Blind or Severe Vision Impairment	660.1	0.6	63.7	74.9	61.7
Deaf or Severe Hearing Impairment	591.4	0.5	70.1	74.5	68.0
Difficulty Walking	2,643.7	2.3	51.6	74.3	63.7
Difficulty Typing	661.8	0.6	58.6	78.7	65.8
Difficulty Leaving Home	891.4	0.8	49.8	77.1	66.7
None of These Disabilities	109,174.8	92.7	69.4	83.4	75.1
Total	117,734.3	100	68.2	82.8	74.4
% not answering	13.4				

Source: NTIA and ESA, U.S. Department of Commerce, using U.S. Census Bureau Current Population Survey Supplements

In an earlier section of this report (see Chapter 6), rates of computer and Internet use were shown to vary substantially by employment status. As shown in Figure 7-1, while people with severely limited sight and hearing have employment rates approaching that of the population that does not have one of these disabilities, people in the other disability categories are much less likely to be employed.

Table 7-4: Internet Activities of 25 to 60 Year-Olds by Disability Status, 2001

	Internet Use from Any Location (%)	Among Internet Users						
		E-Mail or Instant Messaging	Play Games	Search for Product or Service Info.	Purchase Online	News, Weather Sports info	Health Info	Gov. Info
Multiple Disabilities	30.3	84.9	39.8	76.8	41.6	68.0	56.1	39.1
Blind or Severe Vision Impairment	51.5	86.8	46.6	81.9	53.1	73.2	38.7	30.9
Deaf or Severe Hearing Impairment	54.8	84.3	36.5	72.6	48.1	69.4	33.6	32.9
Difficulty Walking	39.8	85.0	41.6	75.5	44.4	66.9	48.2	34.9
Difficulty Typing	49.2	87.6	36.2	79.8	54.8	63.5	51.9	41.8
Difficulty Leaving Home	40.4	84.9	31.5	73.2	45.2	64.5	50.6	38.1
None of These Disabilities	63.1	88.3	32.0	78.5	50.4	70.2	39.1	34.4
Total	61.4	88.2	32.3	78.4	50.2	70.1	39.6	34.5

Source: NTIA and ESA, U.S. Department of Commerce, using U.S. Census Bureau Current Population Survey Supplements

People who are not employed fall into one of two major categories: unemployed (which means that one is in the labor force, but is not employed) and out of the labor force (not looking for a job). The CPS records those not in the labor force as retired, disabled, or other. Overall, 78.6 percent of the population between ages 25 and 60 is employed, 3.1 percent is unemployed, 2.6 percent is retired, 4.9 percent is "disabled," and 10.8 percent fall into the "other" category.[33]

---

[33] These are the percentages for the subset of the population that answered the disability question—13.4 percent of the respondents in this age category did not answer these questions. However, the distribution of this subset does not differ in any meaningful way from the population as a whole. For example, the comparable figure for percent employed in the 25 to 60 age group is 78.6 percent when calculated for the population as a whole.

Figure 7-1: Employment Rates Among 25 to 60 Year-Olds by Disability Status, as a Percent of U.S. Population, 2001

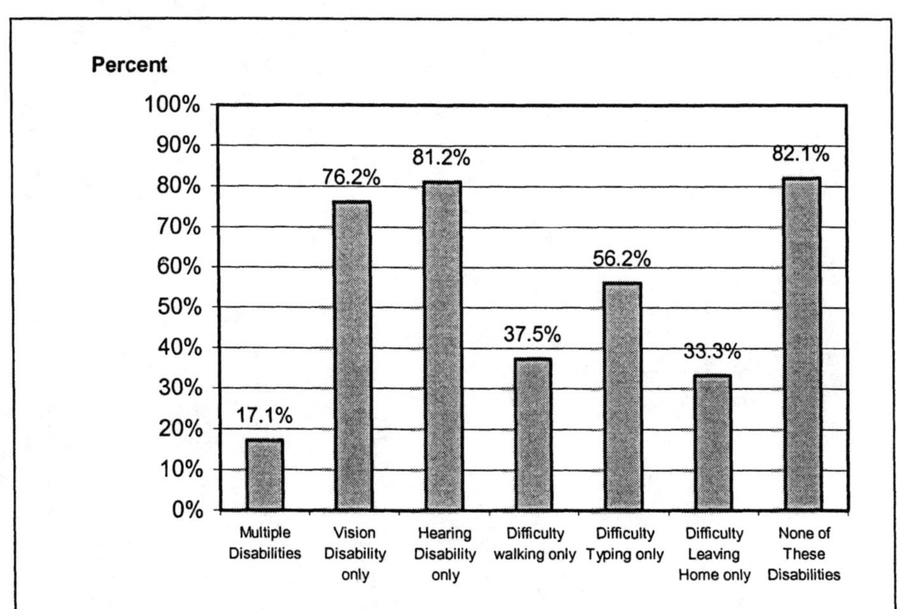

Source: NTIA and ESA, U.S. Department of Commerce, using U.S. Census Bureau Current Population Survey Supplements

The data are sufficient to provide a comparison of persons who gave "disability" as the reason they were not in the labor force for some of the disability categories.[34] Of the disabilities considered here, it is not surprising that those with more than one of the disabilities were the most likely to be out of the labor force for reasons of disability. People with mobility issues (both the "difficulty walking or climbing stairs" and the "inability to leave the house to go to an appointment") also had high rates of being out of the labor force due to disability. As shown in Figure 7-2, 1.8 percent of individuals who replied negatively to the five specific disability questions contained in Box 1 are not in the labor force due to a disability. People with vision or hearing issues are much less likely to be out of the labor force because of their disability.

---

[34] It is not possible to consider the employed/unemployed rates among those with at least one of the disabilities considered here because of limited sample size.

**Figure 7-2: "Not in the Labor Force Because of Disability"
Among 25 to 60 Year-Olds by Disability Status, 2001**

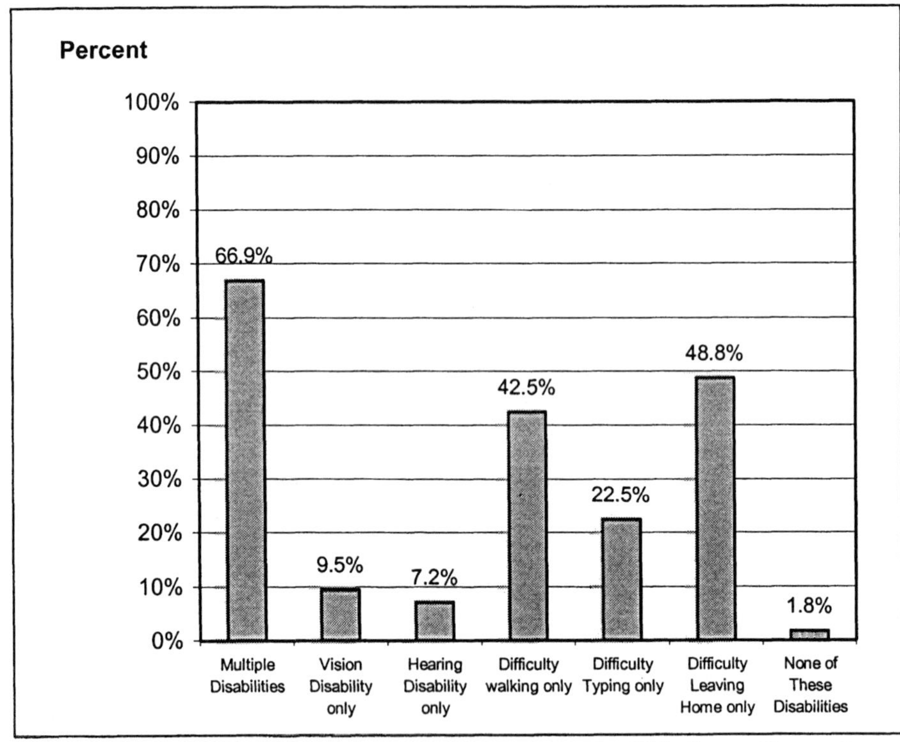

Source: NTIA and ESA, U.S. Department of Commerce, using U.S. Census Bureau Current Population Survey Supplements

On the job, people with either a vision or hearing disability or with multiple disabilities are less likely to use a computer at work than others (Table 7-5). Even among those that do use a computer, substantial differences remain in the extent to which they connect to the Internet or use e-mail. One interesting finding is that the disability category showing the highest rate of on-the-job computer use are those persons who report "having a condition that makes it difficult to type on an ordinary typewriter or traditional computer keyboard." This group has work computer use rates similar to that of the population without one of these disabilities. However, given the fact that 22.5 percent of people in this category are employed in administrative positions where the incidence of repetitive motion disorders such as carpal tunnel syndrome may be high, makes this finding less surprising.

**Table 7-5: Computer and Internet Use at Work Among
Employed 25 to 60 Year-Olds By Disability Status, 2001**

	Uses a Computer at Work (%)	Of Those Who Use a Computer at Work: Uses the Internet at Work (%)
Multiple Disabilities	48.1	68.2
Blind or Severe Vision Impairment	52.1	69.6
Deaf or Severe Hearing Impairment	50.3	57.5
Difficulty Walking	55.4	69.0
Difficulty Typing	58.6	67.9
Difficulty Leaving Home	57.6	71.9
None of These Disabilities	58.4	74.0
Total	58.2	73.8

Source: NTIA and ESA, U.S. Department of Commerce, using U.S. Census Bureau Current Population Survey Supplements

Over 60 Year-Olds

In general, those over age 60 are less likely than other age groups to have a computer in their home or to use the PC or the Internet in the home and for those with a disability the use rates are even lower (Table 7-5). In addition, people in this age group are much less likely to use the Internet outside of the home. For example, the difference between Internet use from home and Internet use from any location was 13.4 percent among those between 3 and 24 who have difficulty walking or climbing stairs (a rise from 32.6 percent to 46.0 percent). The comparable change was only 2.0 percent for the population over 60 with a similar disability (14.1 percent who use the Internet from home to 16.1 percent who use the Internet from any location).

The Interaction of Disability with Computer and Internet Use

The charts and tables above are suggestive that people with disabilities tend to use computers and the Internet at rates below the average for the population. From these tables, however, it is not possible to discern whether other factors, such as education or income, are actually the variables driving the disparity, rather than the fact of the disability. However, statistical analysis indicates that even when income, education, and age are accounted for, people with disabilities considered here are less likely than those without disabilities to be Internet users.[35]

Table 7-5: Computer and Internet Use at Home among Those Over 60 By Disability Status, 2001

	Size of Population in Category (000s)	Percent of Population (%)	Has a Computer at Home (%)	Of Those Who Have a Computer at Home		Uses the Internet from Any Location
				Uses a the Computer at Home (%)	Uses the Internet at Home (%)	
Multiple Disabilities	4,927.2	13.5	22.2	31.4	23.8	6.2
Blind or Severe Vision Impairment	446.7	1.2	30.2	42.6	27.5	9.6
Deaf or Severe Hearing Impairment	771.6	2.1	35.4	56.5	45.7	17.8
Difficulty Walking	2,592.9	7.1	28.7	62.9	49.3	16.1
Difficulty Typing	327.9	0.9	24.9	62.3	52.3	13.5
Difficulty Leaving Home	712.2	2.0	25.7	33.2	25.2	7.2
None of These Disabilities	26,767.1	73.2	39.4	67.0	56.7	25.4
Total	36,545.6		35.8	62.8	52.5	21.3
% not answering	11.4					

Source: NTIA and ESA, U.S. Department of Commerce, using U.S. Census Bureau Current Population Survey Supplements

---

[35] In order to explore this question, a logit regression was run with Internet use from any location as the dependent variable and disability status (dummy variables for each of the disability questions, excluding difficulty leaving home), race dummies, and ordered variables for age, income, and education. A variety of income and education variables were considered and results were robust. The disability variables were uniformly negative and significant, except for one case where dummy variable for multiple disabilities was insignificant.

Chapter 8

THE UNCONNECTED

The earlier chapters of this report have chronicled changes in the connected population: who they are, where they are, what they are doing online, what devices and connection types they are using, and where they are using the Internet. There is a sizable segment of the U.S. population (as of September 2001, 46.1 percent of persons and 49.5 percent of households), however, that does not use the Internet. This chapter profiles this "unconnected" population and explores some of the reasons why it may not be online.

THE OFFLINE POPULATION

Table 8-1 at the end of this chapter presents the complement to Table 2-2—descriptive statistics for those individuals who do not use the Internet. As the analysis in Chapter 2 shows, Internet use has expanded dramatically in the United States, but a number of groups are more likely not to be Internet users. These non-users include:

- People in households with low family incomes — 75.0 percent of people who live in households where income is less than $15,000 and 66.6 percent of those in households with incomes between $15,000 and $35,000.
- Adults with low levels of overall education—60.2 percent of adults (age 25 +) with only a high school degree and 87.2 percent of adults with less than a high school education.[36]

---

[36] A person's level of education is correlated to his/her income. People with low overall levels of education are more likely to live in households with lower family incomes. Levels of educational

- Hispanics—68.4 percent of all Hispanics and 85.9 percent of Hispanic households where Spanish is the only language spoken.
- Blacks—60.2 percent of Blacks.

Earlier chapters have examined the change in the online population focusing on the growth in the number of users or home connections. We gain a different perspective by looking at the rate of *decrease* in the population that is not online. In other words, we compare the change in the online population with the group initially *not online* instead of the group initially online.

Consider in the non-Internet-using population by educational attainment, for example. Among people at least 25 years old with a high school education, the share not using the Internet declined from 69.4 percent in August 2000 to 60.2 in September 2001. Over the same period and age level, the share of those with a college education who were not using the Internet shrank from 27.5 percent to 19.2 percent (Figure 8-1). Thus, high school graduates had a slightly larger point change (9.2 percentage points) than college grads (8.3 percentage points). Because so many more high school grads were not Internet users in August 2000, the 9.2 percentage point change over the next 13 months represented a 12 percent annual rate of decline in non-Internet-users (Table 8-2). On the other hand, so few college grads were non-Internet-users in 2000 that their 8.2 percentage point change reflected a 28 percent annual rate of decline in non-Internet-users. When Chapter 2 examined those same point changes from the perspective of the growth in Internet users, high school grads had a larger growth rate of Internet users than college grads (27 percent vs. 11 percent) (See Table 2-3).

This observation applies to other comparisons. For example, the group of non-users (25 years and older) with less than a high-school degree declined only 4 percent annually while those with a college degree -- a much smaller group -- dropped 27 percent on an annual basis (Table 8-1). The percentage point differences vary similarly.

---

attainment have also increased over time; thus, age and education may be negatively correlated at the higher age levels.

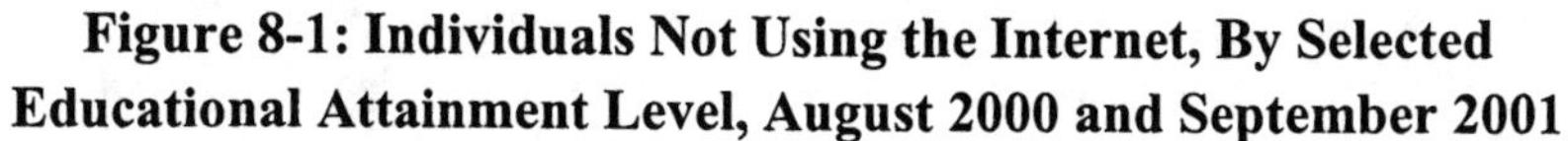

Figure 8-1: Individuals Not Using the Internet, By Selected Educational Attainment Level, August 2000 and September 2001

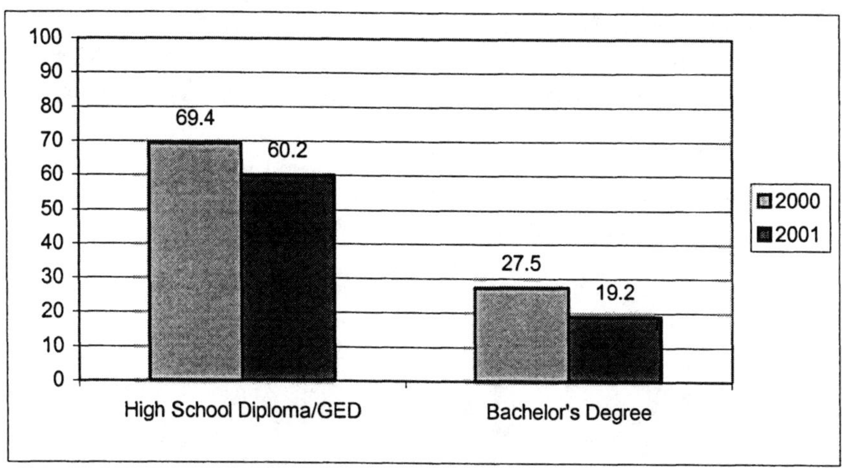

Source: NTIA and ESA, U.S. Department of Commerce, using U.S. Census Bureau Current Population Survey Supplements

THE IMPORTANCE OF COST TO HOUSEHOLDS NEVER CONNECTED TO THE INTERNET

The cost of Internet access matters much more to households with lower incomes than to those with higher incomes. The September 2001 survey asked households without Internet subscriptions the question, "What is the main reason that you don't have the Internet at home?"[37] Survey results indicated that the largest specific response was that the cost was "too expensive."[38] This response was volunteered by one-fourth of these households, but much more often by lower income households than by higher income households.

Figure 8-2 shows the relationship between costs, income, and adoption of home Internet connections. With successively higher income categories, fewer households report that cost is a barrier and more households are making their first connections to the Internet at home. Households with incomes below $15,000 volunteered cost as

---

[37] Tables 8-2a and 8-2b provide summary data by demographic category for those responding households that have never been connected to the Internet and those that have disconnected, respectively.

[38] Approximately one-half of the households who had never subscribed to the Internet at home responded with the ambiguous catchall "don't want it." That response could come from people who have not connected for a combination of specific reasons in addition to those persons who can see no use for it under any conditions, including zero cost.

the barrier to home Internet subscriptions 34.7 percent of the time. Among households in that income category, the share of the population without home Internet subscriptions declined by only 6 percent between August 2000 and September 2001. At the other end of the spectrum, only 9.6 percent of households with incomes of at least $75,000 said that they were deterred by cost. That income level saw a 34 percent reduction in the share of households without home Internet between August 2000 and September 2001.

Figure 8-2: Adoption Rate and Internet "Too Expensive" by Income Percent of U.S. Households without Internet

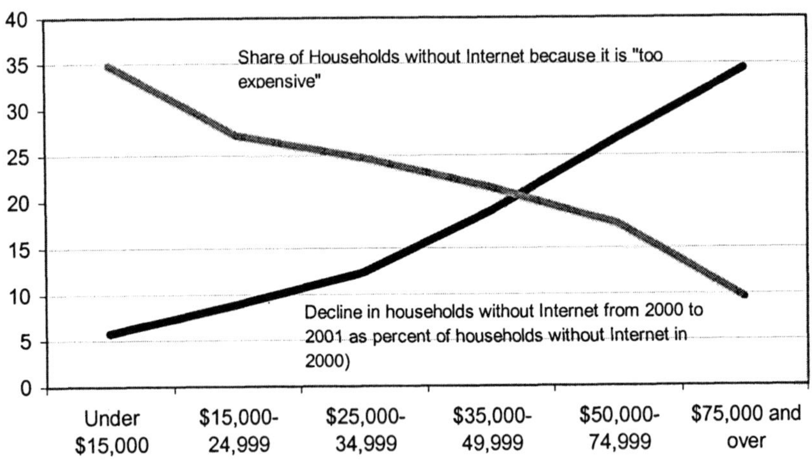

Source: NTIA and ESA, U.S. Department of Commerce, using U.S. Census Bureau Current Population Survey Supplements

Among specific responses, cost rated highly across a number of demographic groups of non-Internet households. In particular, respondents for married couples or single-parent families with children, and heads of households that were younger than 45 years of age, less educated, or unemployed all identified "too expensive" as the most important reason for non-connectivity at a much higher level than the national figure of 25.3 percent.

WHY HOUSEHOLDS HAVE
DISCONTINUED INTERNET ACCESS

Those households that have discontinued Internet access numbered 3.6 million, or 3.3 percent of all U.S. households as of September 2001. Among this group of unconnected persons, cost was the most frequently cited reason for disconnecting. (Figure 8-3) Households with incomes less than $50,000 identified "too expensive" as the primary reason for discontinuing their Internet connection (26.9 percent of such households). Cost was more important in households with only high school degrees (24.6 percent) than in households with college degrees (13.7 percent). Those household heads younger than 45 rated cost (24.2 percent) more highly than households heads 45 years or older (19.0 percent). Geographic differentials existed: households in rural areas cited cost less often (19.9 percent) than households in central cities (25.5 percent).

The lack of a computer or problems with the home computer also accounted for many persons discontinuing their use (Figure 8-3). Although people have concerns about their children's exposure to inappropriate material on the Internet (see discussion at the end of this chapter), this was seldom the reason cited by people who no longer subscribed to the Internet.

Figure 8-3: Reasons for U.S. Households
Discontinuing Internet Access Percent Distribution, 2001

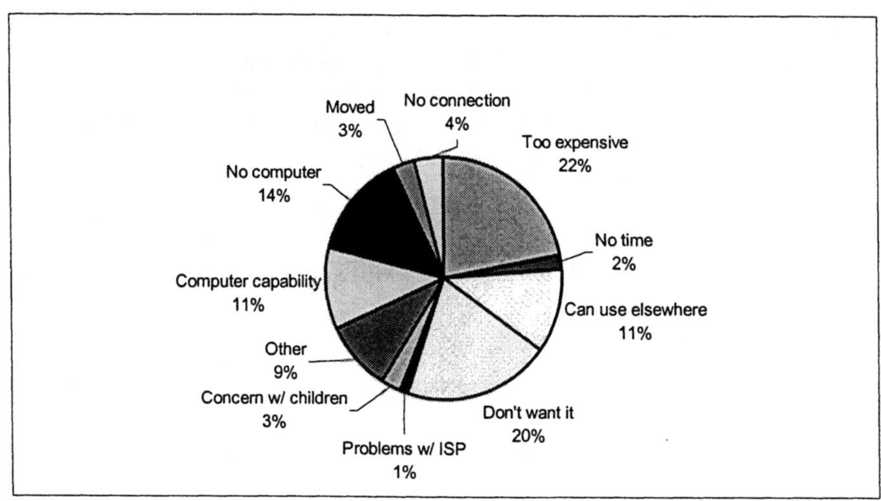

Source: NTIA and ESA, U.S. Department of Commerce, using U.S. Census Bureau Current Population Survey Supplements.

EFFECT OF CONFIDENTIALITY CONCERNS

Some households may choose not to have a home Internet connection because of confidentiality concerns. The September 2001 survey asked respondents if they were more or less concerned about their confidentiality over the Internet as compared to the telephone. It is important to note that although respondents reported being more concerned about their confidentially over the Internet, the question was phrased in such a way that respondents did not rate the degree of concern but rather whether they were more or less concerned.[39]

About half (50.9 percent) of respondents were more concerned about their confidentiality over the Internet compared with the telephone. About one-third (41.4 percent) of respondents reported their concerns were the same for both mediums, and 7.7 percent of respondents reported feeling less concern about confidentiality over the Internet compared to on a telephone.

In terms of age, persons under 25 year olds were the least concerned about their confidentiality over the Internet (36.0 percent), compared with those 55 years of age or older who were the most concerned (54.8 percent). A majority of respondents in the two age groups under 35 reported that they were either neutral or more concerned about the telephone. In contrast, a majority of respondents over 35 were more concerned about the Internet than were either neutral or more concerned about the telephone. Examining gender revealed that females and males shared a similar level of concern about confidentiality over the Internet: 51.8 percent compared to 50.1 percent, respectively. Looking at household types, male-led households were least likely to be concerned about confidentiality over the Internet (41.4 percent), while female-led households were most concerned (54.9 percent). Male-led households were also most likely to respond that there was no difference in confidentiality between the two mediums (52.5 percent), compared to 38.0 percent of female-led household who reported that there was no difference.

CONTENT CONCERNS

Some households, particularly those with children under the age of 18, may choose not to have a home Internet connection because of the concern that the children may access inappropriate material. As discussed in Chapter 5, the September 2001 survey found that among households with children, 68.3 percent

---

[39] The specific question reads: "Compared to providing information over the telephone, how concerned are you about providing personal information over the Internet? Are you: (1) more concerned (2) less concerned (3) about the same."

responded that compared with material on television, they were more concerned about the kind of material children may be exposed to on the Internet. This concern, however, did not translate into lower rates of Internet access among this group. Among those that thought the Internet was a source of more concern than television, 51.8 percent had Internet in the home as compared to 48.2 percent who did not subscribe to the Internet. Those who were less concerned (5.6 percent) or had similar concerns (26.1 percent) actually constituted a lower proportion of Internet households.

THE ROLE OF NETWORK EFFECTS

"Network effects" may be another factor determining whether people connect to the Internet.[40] Typically, the adoption of a technology that has "network effects" begins slowly. At some point a successful technology will reach a tipping point and adoption will accelerate rapidly. As the technology saturates the market, the adoption rate slows, since most people who want the technology already have it.[41]

Generally, the adoption of a technology does not take place uniformly across the entire economy or the entire population. The penetration rate for fax machines, for example, is much higher among businesses than among households. The fax never rivaled the telephone or mail for household communications, whereas businesses found considerable value in the near instant transmission of documents. Under this concept, if a person's family, friends, and broader community are Internet users, there would be increased incentive for them to go online. On the other hand, if few of a person's family, friends, or community were online, there would be less of an incentive to go online. In looking at the relationship of home Internet to variables such as income, education, race or Hispanic origin, we may be picking up in part the probability of family, friends, and community to be online.

In sum, there are a number of reasons as to why a substantial proportion of U.S. households do not currently use the Internet. Some reasons, such as those related to "network effects," can be surmised from adoption patterns of new technologies. Other reasons were provided as rationale in the September 2001 survey. Cost ("too expensive") rates highest among lower-income households, particularly for those that have decided to discontinue Internet access at home, and highly among many demographic groups of non-Internet households. In contrast, confidentiality issues (even where households express greater concerns about the Internet than television)

---

[40] "Network effects" (also called "network externality") centers on the notion that the addition of another subscriber in a network increases the value of access to existing or potential subscribers,

[41] This pattern is characterized by an "S" curve. For a more detailed discussion, see U.S. Department of Commerce, *Falling Through The Net:* **Toward Digital Inclusion**, pp. 2-4.

and concerns about how children use the Internet do not appear to be significant reasons why households stay or go offline.

Table 8-1: Non-Internet Use From Any Location by Individuals Age 3 and Older, October 1997, December 1998, August 2000, and September 2001

	Oct. 1997 (thousands)		Dec. 1998 (thousands)		Aug. 2000 (thousands)		Sept. 2001 (thousands)		Non-Internet Use (percent of population)			
	Non-Internet Users	Total	Non-Internet Users	Total	Non-Internet Users	Total	Non-Internet Users	Total	Oct. 1997	Dec. 1998	Aug. 2000	Sept. 2001
Total Population	198,914	255,689	173,866	258,453	146,140	262,620	122,357	265,180	77.8	67.3	55.6	46.1
Gender												
Male	94,279	124,590	82,899	125,932	70,882	127,844	59,572	129,152	75.7	65.8	55.4	46.1
Female	104,635	131,099	90,966	132,521	75,258	134,776	62,785	136,028	79.8	68.6	55.8	46.2
Race/ Origin												
White	137,617	184,295	115,510	184,980	92,725	186,439	74,851	186,793	74.7	62.4	49.7	40.1
Black	27,589	31,786	26,012	32,123	23,226	32,850	20,068	33,305	86.8	81.0	70.7	60.2
Asian Amer. & Pac. Isl.	6,794	9,225	6,221	9,688	5,229	10,324	4,223	10,674	73.6	64.2	50.6	39.6
Hispanic	25,133	28,233	24,556	29,452	23,593	30,918	22,005	32,146	89.0	83.4	76.3	68.4
Employment Status												
Employed[b]	93,603	130,857	76,580	133,119	59,073	136,044	46,693	135,089	71.5	57.5	43.4	34.6
Not Employed[b, d]	63,899	72,911	58,890	73,151	52,570	73,891	48,736	77,268	87.6	80.5	71.1	63.1
Family Income												
Less than $15,000	40,215	44,284	32,694	37,864	26,039	32,096	23,506	31,354	90.8	86.3	81.1	75.0
$15,000 - $24,999	28,662	32,423	24,958	30,581	20,664	27,727	17,756	26,649	88.4	81.6	74.5	66.6
$25,000 - $34,999	27,512	33,178	23,786	31,836	19,947	31,001	15,980	28,571	82.9	74.7	64.3	55.9
$35,000 - $49,999	29,953	38,776	25,498	39,026	19,177	35,867	15,457	36,044	77.2	65.3	53.5	42.9
$50,000 - $74,999	28,358	41,910	23,874	43,776	18,392	43,451	14,621	44,692	67.7	54.5	42.3	32.7
$75,000 & above	20,296	36,572	17,360	42,221	15,625	52,189	11,900	56,446	55.5	41.1	29.9	21.1

	Oct. 1997 (thousands)		Dec. 1998 (thousands)		Aug. 2000 (thousands)		Sept. 2001 (thousands)		Non-Internet Use (percent of population)			
	Non-Internet Users	Total	Non-Internet Users	Total	Non-Internet Users	Total	Non-Internet Users	Total	Oct. 1997	Dec. 1998	Aug. 2000	Sept. 2001
Educational Attainment												
Less Than High School [a]	28,598	29,114	27,811	29,039	25,773	28,254	23,977	27,484	98.2	95.8	91.2	87.2
High School Diploma/GED [a]	51,898	57,487	46,142	57,103	39,463	56,889	34,539	57,386	90.3	80.8	69.4	60.2
Some College [a]	31,995	42,544	26,435	43,038	20,427	44,628	17,099	45,420	75.2	61.4	45.8	37.6
Bachelors Degree [a]	16,291	27,795	12,054	28,990	8,351	30,329	5,863	30,588	58.6	41.6	27.5	19.2
Beyond Bachelors Degree [a]	6,668	13,863	4,884	14,518	3,322	15,426	2,650	16,283	48.1	33.6	21.5	16.3
Age Group (and Labor Force)												
Age 3 – 8	22,697	24,445	21,602	24,282	20,291	23,962	17,126	23,763	92.8	89.0	84.7	72.1
Age 9 – 17	23,678	35,469	20,425	35,821	17,094	36,673	11,638	37,118	66.8	57.0	46.6	31.4
Age 18 – 24	17,088	24,973	14,306	25,662	11,419	26,458	9,464	27,137	68.4	55.7	43.2	34.9
Age 25 – 49	74,214	101,853	60,142	101,836	45,513	101,946	36,752	101,890	72.9	59.1	44.6	36.1
Male	35,498	50,177	29,165	50,054	22,956	50,034	19,128	50,020	70.7	58.3	45.9	38.2
Female	38,716	51,676	30,975	51,781	22,557	51,913	17,624	51,871	74.9	59.8	43.5	34.0
Age 50 +	61,237	68,949	57,183	70,852	51,822	73,580	47,377	75,272	88.8	80.7	70.4	62.9
Male	26,692	31,252	24,892	32,248	22,572	33,561	20,681	34,438	85.4	77.2	67.3	60.1
Female	34,545	37,697	32,291	38,604	29,250	40,019	26,696	40,834	91.6	83.6	73.1	65.4
Geographic Location of Household In Which the Individual Lives												
Rural	n/a	n/a	46,554	65,828	39,091	67,980	31,891	67,642	n/a	70.7	57.5	47.1
Urban	n/a	n/a	127,312	192,625	107,049	194,640	90,465	197,537	n/a	66.1	55.0	45.8
Urban Not Central City	n/a	n/a	74,210	116,091	61,868	118,641	51,382	120,724	n/a	63.9	52.1	42.6
Urban Central City	n/a	n/a	53,102	76,534	45,181	75,999	39,083	76,813	n/a	69.4	59.4	50.9

	Oct. 1997 (thousands)		Dec. 1998 (thousands)		Aug. 2000 (thousands)		Sept. 2001 (thousands)		Non-Internet Use (percent of population)			
	Non-Internet Users	Total	Non-Internet Users	Total	Non-Internet Users	Total	Non-Internet Users	Total	Oct. 1997	Dec. 1998	Aug. 2000	Sept. 2001
Household Type In Which the Individual Lives												
Married Couple w/Children <18 Years Old	76,127	103,791	68,833	110,295	55,798	112,920	39,623	104,337	73.3	62.4	49.4	38.0
Male Householder w/Children <18 Years Old	5,141	6,284	5,871	7,866	5,361	8,186	4,011	7,400	81.8	74.6	65.5	54.2
Female Householder w/Children <18 Years Old	23,286	27,327	21,658	27,877	20,168	30,034	15,892	29,032	85.2	77.7	67.2	54.7
Family Household without Children <18 Years Old	62,373	77,612	50,495	72,155	41,322	70,521	40,599	81,996	80.4	70.0	58.6	49.5
Non-Family Household	31,088	39,381	26,979	40,199	23,442	40,884	22,196	42,333	78.9	67.1	57.3	52.4

Source: U.S. Bureau of the Census, Current Population Survey supplements, October 1997, December 1998, August 2000, September 2001.
Notes: [a] Age 25 and older. [b] Age 16 and Older. [c] Individuals who live in households in which the answer to the question "Is Spanish the only language spoken by all members of the household who are 15 years of age or older?" was yes. [d] Both people who are unemployed and people not in the labor force.

Table 8-2: Percent Difference and Growth Rates Non-Internet Use From Any Location by Individuals Age 3 and Older, October 1997, December 1998, August 2000, and September 2001

	Non-Internet Use (percent of population)				Percentage Point Difference				Decline in Non-Use Rate (annual rate)			
	Oct. 1997*	Dec. 1998	Aug. 2000	Sept. 2001	1997 to 1998*	1998 to 2000	2000 to 2001	1998 to 2001	1997 to 1998*	1998 to 2000	2000 to 2001	1998 to 2001
Total Population	77.8	67.3	55.6	46.1	n/a	-11.6	-9.5	-21.1	n/a	11	16	13
Gender												
Male	75.7	65.8	55.4	46.1	n/a	-10.4	-9.3	-19.7	n/a	10	16	12
Female	79.8	68.6	55.8	46.2	n/a	-12.8	-9.7	-22.5	n/a	12	16	13
Race/ Origin												
White	74.7	62.4	49.7	40.1	n/a	-12.7	-9.7	-22.4	n/a	13	18	15
Black	86.8	81.0	70.7	60.2	n/a	-10.3	-10.4	-20.7	n/a	8	14	10
Asian Amer. & Pac. Isl.	73.6	64.2	50.6	39.6	n/a	-13.6	-11.1	-24.7	n/a	13	20	16
Hispanic	89.0	83.4	76.3	68.4	n/a	-7.1	-7.9	-14.9	n/a	5	10	7
Employment Status												
Employed [b]	71.5	57.5	43.4	34.6	n/a	-14.1	-8.9	-23.0	n/a	16	19	17
Not Employed [b, c]	87.6	80.5	71.1	63.1	n/a	-9.4	-8.1	-17.4	n/a	7	11	8
Family Income												
Less than $15,000	90.8	86.3	81.1	75.0	n/a	-5.2	-6.2	-11.4	n/a	4	7	5
$15,000 - $24,999	88.4	81.6	74.5	66.6	n/a	-7.1	-7.9	-15.0	n/a	5	10	7
$25,000 - $34,999	82.9	74.7	64.3	55.9	n/a	-10.4	-8.4	-18.8	n/a	9	12	10
$35,000 - $49,999	77.2	65.3	53.5	42.9	n/a	-11.9	-10.6	-22.5	n/a	11	18	14
$50,000 - $74,999	67.7	54.5	42.3	32.7	n/a	-12.2	-9.6	-21.8	n/a	14	21	17
$75,000 & above	55.5	41.1	29.9	21.1	n/a	-11.2	-8.9	-20.0	n/a	17	28	22

	Non-Internet Use (percent of population)				Percentage Point Difference				Decline in Non-Use Rate (annual rate)			
	Oct. 1997*	Dec. 1998	Aug. 2000	Sept. 2001	1997 to 1998*	1998 to 2000	2000 to 2001	1998 to 2001	1997 to 1998*	1998 to 2000	2000 to 2001	1998 to 2001
Educational Attainment												
Less Than High School [a]	98.2	95.8	91.2	87.2	n/a	-4.6	-4.0	-8.5	n/a	3	4	3
High School Diploma / GED [a]	90.3	80.8	69.4	60.2	n/a	-11.4	-9.2	-20.6	n/a	9	12	10
Some College [a]	75.2	61.4	45.8	37.6	n/a	-15.7	-8.1	-23.8	n/a	16	17	16
Bachelors Degree [a]	58.6	41.6	27.5	19.2	n/a	-14.0	-8.4	-22.4	n/a	22	28	25
Beyond Bachelors Degree [a]	48.1	33.6	21.5	16.3	n/a	-12.1	-5.3	-17.4	n/a	23	23	23
Age Group (and Labor Force)												
Age 3 – 8	92.8	89.0	84.7	72.1	n/a	-4.3	-12.6	-16.9	n/a	3	14	7
Age 9 – 17	66.8	57.0	46.6	31.4	n/a	-10.4	-15.3	-25.7	n/a	11	31	20
Age 18 – 24	68.4	55.7	43.2	34.9	n/a	-12.6	-8.3	-20.9	n/a	14	18	16
Age 25 – 49	72.9	59.1	44.6	36.1	n/a	-14.4	-8.6	-23.0	n/a	15	18	16
Male	70.7	58.3	45.9	38.2	n/a	-12.4	-7.6	-20.0	n/a	13	15	14
Female	74.9	59.8	43.5	34.0	n/a	-16.4	-9.5	-25.8	n/a	17	20	19
Age 50 +	88.8	80.7	70.4	62.9	n/a	-10.3	-7.5	-17.8	n/a	8	10	9
Male	85.4	77.2	67.3	60.1	n/a	-9.9	-7.2	-17.1	n/a	8	10	9
Female	91.6	83.6	73.1	65.4	n/a	-10.6	-7.7	-18.3	n/a	8	10	9
Geographic Location of Household In Which the Individual Lives												
Rural	n/a	70.7	57.5	47.1	n/a	-13.2	-10.4	-23.6	n/a	12	17	14
Urban	n/a	66.1	55.0	45.8	n/a	-11.1	-9.2	-20.3	n/a	10	16	12
Urban Not Central City	n/a	63.9	52.1	42.6	n/a	-11.8	-9.6	-21.4	n/a	12	17	14
Urban Central City	n/a	69.4	59.4	50.9	n/a	-9.9	-8.6	-18.5	n/a	9	13	11

	Non-Internet Use (percent of population)				Percentage Point Difference				Decline in Non-Use Rate (annual rate)			
	Oct. 1997*	Dec. 1998	Aug. 2000	Sept. 2001	1997 to 1998*	1998 to 2000	2000 to 2001	1998 to 2001	1997 to 1998*	1998 to 2000	2000 to 2001	1998 to 2001
Household Type In Which the Individual Lives												
Married Couple w/Children <18 Years Old	73.3	62.4	49.4	38.0	n/a	-13.0	-11.4	-24.4	n/a	13	22	17
Male Householder w/Children <18 Years Old	81.8	74.6	65.5	54.2	n/a	-9.1	-11.3	-20.4	n/a	8	16	11
Female Householder w/Children <18 Years Old	85.2	77.7	67.2	54.7	n/a	-10.5	-12.4	-23.0	n/a	8	17	12
Family Household without Children <18 Years Old	80.4	70.0	58.6	49.5	n/a	-11.4	-9.1	-20.5	n/a	10	14	12
Non-Family Household	78.9	67.1	57.3	52.4	n/a	-9.8	-4.9	-14.7	n/a	9	8	9

Source: U.S. Bureau of the Census, Current Population Survey supplements, October 1997, December 1998, August 2000, September 2001.
Notes: *The October 1997 question on Internet usage was worded considerably differently than the questions used in the following years. The use rates calculated from the October 1997 data are likely correct in terms of their order of magnitude. Growth rates have, however, not been calculated because the implied precision of the year-to-year comparisons would be inaccurate. [a] Age 25 and older. [b] Age 16 and Older. [c] Both people who are unemployed and people not in the labor force.

Table 8-3: Main Reasons for No Internet Use at Home, by Selected Characteristics of Reference Person (Numbers in Thousands) Total USA, 2001

	Total Households	Don't Want It		Too Expensive		Can Use Elsewhere		Concerned About Children Using It	
		No.	%	No.	%	No.	%	No.	%
All Households	49,197	26,100	53.05	12,443	25.29	2,010	4.09	456	0.93
Family Income									
Under $5,000	2,214	852	38.47	941	42.47	65	2.95	6	0.25
$5,000 - $9,999	4,906	2,409	49.09	1,647	33.58	72	1.47	20	0.42
$10,000 - $14,999	5,537	2,847	51.41	1,809	32.68	77	1.39	15	0.26
$15,000 - $19,999	3,750	1,953	52.08	1,032	27.53	77	2.05	35	0.94
$20,000 - $24,999	4,374	2,264	51.75	1,168	26.69	145	3.30	41	0.93
$25,000 - $34,999	6,300	3,263	51.79	1,569	24.90	281	4.46	71	1.12
$35,000 - $49,999	5,519	2,858	51.79	1,194	21.64	372	6.74	87	1.58
$50,000 - $74,999	3,976	2,056	51.71	707	17.78	314	7.91	59	1.48
$75,000	2,293	1,236	53.88	219	9.55	330	14.41	50	2.17
Not Reported	10,326	6,363	61.62	2,157	20.89	277	2.68	72	0.70
Age									
Under 25 years old	3,212	972	30.26	1,384	43.10	235	7.30	12	0.38
25-34 years old	6,970	2,262	32.46	2,803	40.21	497	7.13	109	1.56
35-44 years old	7,954	2,971	37.35	2,841	35.71	444	5.58	214	2.69
45-54 years old	7,815	3,752	48.00	2,263	28.96	414	5.30	89	1.13
55+ years old	23,246	16,143	69.44	3,152	13.56	421	1.81	33	0.14

	Total Households	Don't Want It		Too Expensive		Can Use Elsewhere		Concerned About Children Using It	
		No.	%	No.	%	No.	%	No.	%
Race									
White Not Hispanic	32,586	19,276	59.15	6,105	18.74	1,476	4.53	288	0.88
Black Not Hispanic	8,676	3,563	41.06	3,366	38.80	272	3.14	66	0.76
AIEA Not Hispanic	455	180	39.52	158	34.85	20	4.37	5	1.01
API Not Hispanic	1,023	470	45.90	274	26.78	70	6.88	12	1.18
Hispanic	6,456	2,611	40.45	2,539	39.33	172	2.66	85	1.32
Gender									
Male	23,620	13,022	55.13	5,244	22.20	1,021	4.32	249	1.06
Female	25,577	13,077	51.33	7,200	28.15	990	3.87	206	0.81
Educational Attainment									
Elementary: 0-8 years	5,985	3,468	57.95	1,505	25.15	67	1.11	24	0.40
Some High School: no diploma	7,579	4,052	53.46	2,241	29.58	135	1.78	73	0.97
High School Diploma/GED	18,612	10,164	54.61	4,772	25.64	569	3.06	165	0.88
Some College	10,939	5,315	48.59	2,875	26.28	566	5.18	132	1.21
Bachelors Degree or more	6,082	3,101	50.98	1,050	17.26	673	11.07	62	1.02
Household Type									
Married Couple w/Children <18 Years Old	6,556	2,331	35.56	2,388	36.43	285	4.35	319	4.87
Male Householder w/Children <18 Years Old	1,112	370	33.24	489	44.00	30	2.70	12	1.11

	Total Households	Don't Want It		Too Expensive		Can Use Elsewhere		Concerned About Children Using It	
		No.	%	No.	%	No.	%	No.	%
Household Type									
Female Householder w/Children <18 Years Old	5,030	1,176	23.38	2,766	55.00	177	3.53	76	1.51
Family Household without Children <18 Years Old	15,423	9,648	62.56	2,740	17.77	541	3.51	36	0.23
Non-Family Household	21,076	12,575	59.66	4,059	19.26	977	4.63	13	0.06
Employment									
Employed	25,078	11,040	44.02	7,459	29.74	1,699	6.77	356	1.42
Unemployed	1,406	412	29.28	668	47.47	42	2.99	24	1.73
Not in Labor Force	22,713	14,648	64.49	4,317	19.01	269	1.19	76	0.33
Region									
Northwest	9,088	5,116	56.29	2,094	23.05	321	3.53	72	0.80
Midwest	11,557	6,085	52.65	2,684	23.23	538	4.66	106	0.92
South	19,088	10,357	54.35	5,175	27.11	735	3.85	170	0.89
West	9,463	4,523	47.80	2,490	26.31	416	4.39	107	1.14

	Computer Capability		No Computer in Household		Lack of Knowledge		Other	
	No.	%	No.	%	No.	%	No.	%
All Households	520	1.06	2,917	5.93	1,032	2.1	3,718	7.56
Family Income								
Under $5,000	12	0.53	156	7.03	42	1.89	142	6.42
$5,000 - 9,999	12	0.26	250	5.09	204	4.16	291	5.94
$10,000 - $14,999	51	0.93	346	6.26	127	2.29	265	4.79
$15,000 - $19,999	36	0.96	265	7.07	122	3.26	230	6.12
$20,000 - $24,999	62	1.41	312	7.13	100	2.29	284	6.48
$25,000 - $34,999	67	1.07	474	7.52	124	1.97	451	7.16
$35,000 - $49,999	88	1.59	379	6.88	92	1.67	448	8.12
$50,000 - $74,999	85	2.15	298	7.5	51	1.27	405	10.2
$75,000 & above	45	1.97	104	4.53	27	1.19	282	12.31
No Reported	62	0.6	333	3.23	143	1.38	920	8.9
Age								
Under 25 years old	39	1.23	317	9.85	21	0.67	232	7.21
25-34 years old	99	1.43	588	8.44	80	1.14	532	7.64
35-44 years old	146	1.84	570	7.16	104	1.31	664	8.35
45-54 years old	91	1.16	463	5.93	133	1.71	610	7.8
55+ years old	144	0.62	979	4.21	693	2.98	1,680	7.23

	Computer Capability		No Computer in Household		Lack of Knowledge		Other	
	No.	%	No.	%	No.	%	No.	%
Race								
White	360	1.11	1,833	5.62	599	1.84	2,649	8.13
Black	57	0.66	585	6.74	173	2	594	6.84
AIEA Not Hispanic	9	2.08	31	6.82	12	2.55	40	8.81
API Not Hispanic	16	1.59	44	4.3	43	4.18	94	9.19
Hispanic	77	1.2	424	6.57	206	3.19	342	5.29
Gender								
Male	268	1.14	1,334	5.65	516	2.18	1,966	8.32
Female	252	0.98	1,583	6.19	516	2.02	1,752	6.85
Education								
Elementary: 0-8 years	32	0.54	234	3.91	284	4.75	370	6.19
Some High School: no diploma	61	0.81	412	5.43	186	2.46	417	5.51
High School Diploma/GED	156	0.84	1,160	6.23	347	1.87	1,280	6.88
Some College	151	1.38	806	7.37	130	1.19	964	8.82
Bachelors Degree or more	120	1.98	306	5.03	84	1.38	686	11.29

	Computer Capability		No Computer in Household		Lack of Knowledge		Other	
	No.	%	No.	%	No.	%	No.	%
Household Type								
Married Couple w/Children <18 Years Old	149	2.28	448	6.83	88	1.35	547	8.34
Male Householder w/Children <18 Years Old	30	2.66	101	9.08	22	2.01	58	5.2
Female Householder w/Children <18 Years Old	72	1.43	458	9.12	30	0.59	274	5.45
Family Household without Children <18 Years Old	127	0.82	734	4.76	355	2.3	1,242	8.05
Non-Family Household	143	0.68	1,176	5.58	537	2.55	1,598	7.58
Employment								
Employed	382	1.52	1,775	7.08	327	1.31	2,039	8.13
Unemployed	5	0.33	137	9.71	34	2.45	85	6.04
Not in Labor Force	133	0.59	1,006	4.43	670	2.95	1,594	7.02
Region								
Northwest	71	0.78	461	5.07	161	1.77	792	8.72
Midwest	133	1.15	768	6.65	259	2.24	983	8.51
South	160	0.84	951	4.98	395	2.07	1,127	5.9
West	156	1.64	738	7.8	218	2.3	816	8.62

REDUCTIONS IN INEQUALITY FOR COMPUTER AND INTERNET USE

In discussions of changing computer and Internet use, a common question is whether inequality has been rising or declining. While previous chapters in this report show that inequality remains, this chapter shows that inequality has been declining by the standard measure of inequality used by economists. Just as income inequality declines when incomes grow faster among those with lower incomes, inequality in computer and Internet use declines when use rises faster among those with lower rates of use. Earlier chapters have noted that higher rates of growth in both computer and Internet use have been occurring among those groups with lower rates of use, such as those with lower income, with less education, from racial groups with low rates, or over 60 years of age.

Different rates of computer and Internet use result from such factors as income, education, use at school, and use at work in different occupations. Income still matters because computers and Internet subscriptions still cost a significant amount of money. On the other hand, income becomes less a factor as prices of computers and Internet subscriptions decline. For school-age children, we found substantial differences in home access to computers and the Internet according to household income. When school and library use are taken into account, however, differences in computer and Internet use among children were much smaller. Among adults, higher levels of education are associated both with greater income and with occupations that tend to use computers and the Internet at work. Once again, we found that computers and the Internet were becoming more common in occupations with lower rates of use.

How a Gini Coefficient for Computer and Internet Use is Computed

To analyze the distribution of computer and Internet use, we have adapted the standard methodology for assessing the distribution of income. In the case of income inequality, households are ranked according to their income and a Lorenz curve is drawn (starting with the lowest incomes) to indicate the cumulative income received by the cumulative population up to that point. For example, Figure 9-1 depicts the distribution of U.S. money income in 2000. Since the bottom 40 percent of the population received 12.5 percent of income, the Lorenz curve goes through (0.4, 0.125).

The most widely used measure of inequality, the Gini coefficient, derives from the Lorenz curve. A Gini coefficient of 0 means that income is equally distributed among the population, while a value of 1 means essentially one person has all the income while everyone else has none. The Gini coefficient measures the area between the straight line connecting (0,0) and (1,1) and the Lorenz curve connecting those two points, as a proportion of the triangle formed by (0,0), (1,0), and (1,1). The Gini coefficient equals zero in the case of absolute equality because the Lorenz curve would lie along the straight line from (0,0) to (1,1). In a situation of absolute inequality (in which only one person had all income), the Lorenz curve would run from (0,0) along the X axis until virtually (1,0) and then abruptly rise to (1,1).

Figure 9-1: Lorenz Curve of Household Money Income, 2000

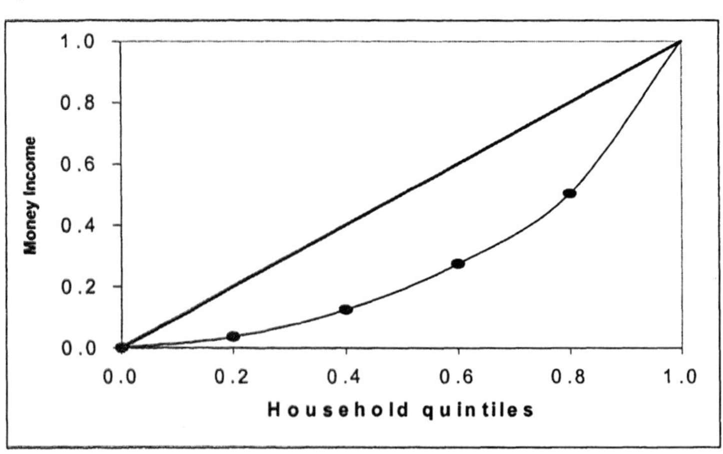

The standard approach to measuring income inequality differs from our approach to measuring inequality of computer and Internet use in one key aspect. In the case of income distribution, virtually every household has income that is reported at a very specific level. In our case, we divide the population into distinct groups (such as by income, education, or occupation) and compute the number of users within each group. Note also that we cannot measure intensity of use. In most of the calculations in this chapter, a person who occasionally uses the Internet at the library is counted the same as someone using a broadband connection for hours a day.

Figure 9-2 shows the distribution of household computer ownership by family income in 1984 and 2001. In 1984, the lowest 42 percent of households by income accounted for only 12 percent of computer users. By 2001, the lowest income 45 percent of households included about 27 percent of computer users. With lower income people accounting for a much higher share of computer users in 2001, the curve for 2001 "bows out" much less than the curve for 1984. The Lorenz curve for 1984 divides the lower right triangle almost in half, for a Gini efficient that year of .438. By 2001, the area between the curve and diagonal was less than a quarter of the triangle, for a Gini coefficient of .229 in 2001. (By comparison, the Gini coefficient for the distribution of money income among households indicated greater inequality, rising from .415 in 1984 to .460 for the most recent year, 2000.)

Figure 9-2: Lorenz Curve for Households with Computers vs. Income

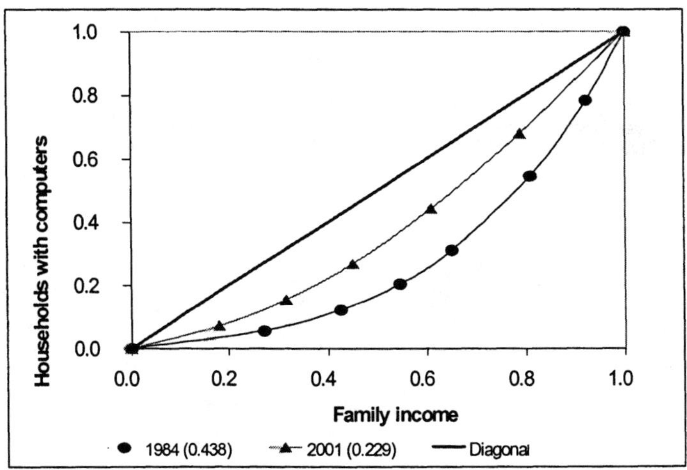

Figure 9-3 traces the descent of the Gini coefficient for household computer ownership beginning in 1984 and continuing through available data points to 2001. The figure shows that, even though significant disparities remain, the distribution of computers among households has moved continuously in the direction of less inequality. Most of the decline occurred in the second half of the period. (By contrast, the Gini coefficient for household money income dispersion went in the other direction, rising from .427 in 1984 to .460 in 2000)

Figure 9-3: Gini Coefficients for Households with Computers, Selected years

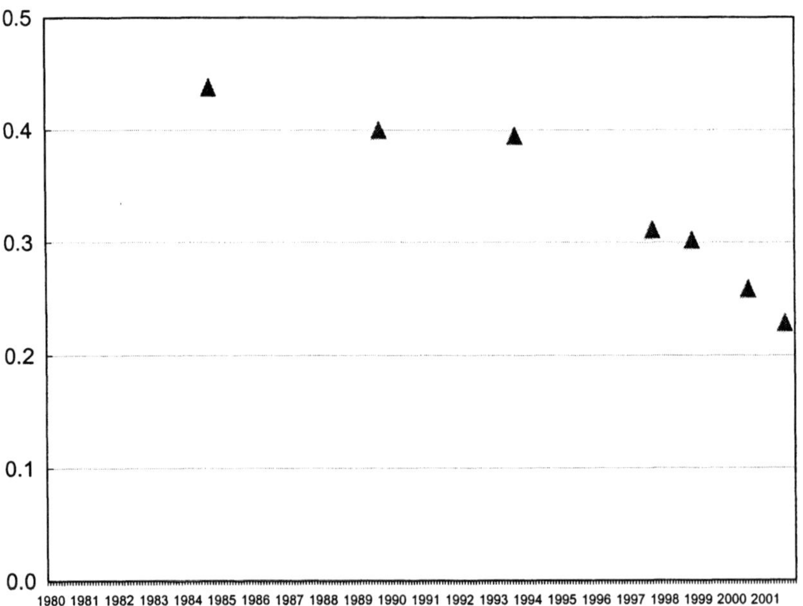

Internet use figures have a shorter history. Even so, whether measured against income, education, family type, or race/ethnicity, the distribution of Internet use at home has moved in the direction of lower inequality. Figures 9-4 and 9-5 depict the reduction of inequality between 1998 and 2001 in Internet use at home based on income and education categories. In the case of income groups, the Gini coefficient declined from .361 in 1998 to .254 in 2001. For educational attainment groups, the measures of inequality for the two years were almost identical, falling from .364 to .262.

Figure 9-4: Lorenz Curve - Internet Use at home vs. Family income

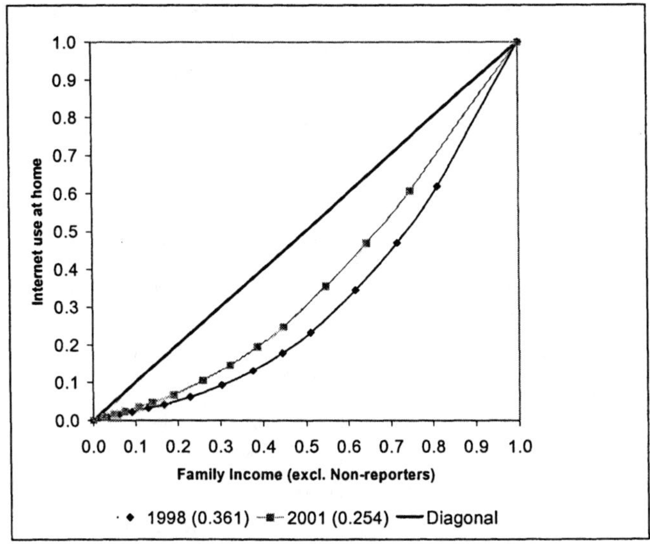

Figure 9-5: Lorenz Curve - Internet Use at home vs. Education

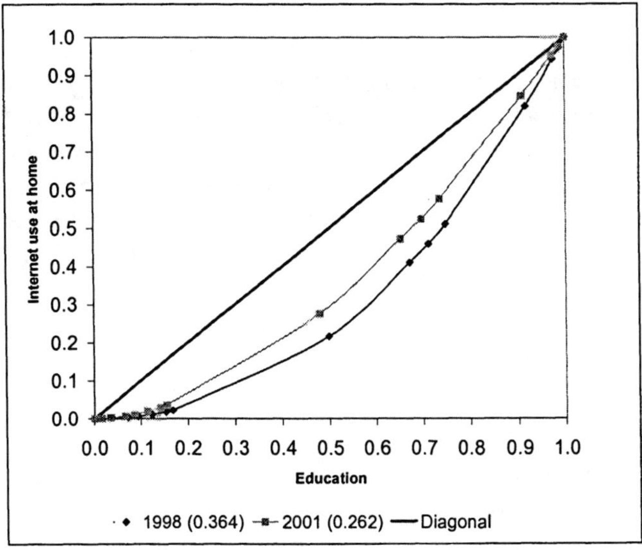

The Gini coefficient may also be used to calibrate the effects of work and school on inequality. Chapter 6 found that, when someone in the household used the Internet at work, there were much smaller disparities in home Internet rates between high and low income households. That lower inequality is reflected by a Gini coefficient of only .083 among households with Internet users at work versus .298 among households in which no one uses the Internet at work.

Digital Workplace (Chapter 6) also noted that the rates of Internet use varied substantially by occupation, but were rising in some occupations that had been lower in 1998. The Gini measure confirms that, with a reduction of inequality by occupation falling from .374 in 1998 to .303 in 2001.

Similarly, Chapter 5 showed a substantial equalizing effect of school on both computer and Internet use compared to use at home. Among 10 to 17 year olds, the Gini coefficient for home computer use was .111 among income groups, but was only .026 for home and school computer use combined. In the case of Internet use, the disparity in home use was larger (.176) and the effect of schools was smaller (down to .124).

These analyses show that substantial changes have occurred since the introduction of both home computers and the Internet when the initial user community tended to be dominated by those who had higher incomes or had them at work or both. The jobs involving computers and the Internet tended to require more education. As a result, inequality based on income and education was substantial. Over time, however, declining prices, increased availability in schools and libraries, and wider applications in many occupations have combined to reduce inequality in both computer and Internet use.

The measure of inequality for broadband fell from 2000 to 2001, but remains notably higher than the measure for home Internet subscriptions generally. The Gini coefficient for broadband declined from .395 in August 2000 to .374 in September 2001. The Gini coefficient for Internet subscriptions overall decreased from .309 to .270 over the same period. Because home broadband service costs substantially more than regular dial-up Internet service, it should come as no surprise that broadband is distributed more towards higher income groups than dial-up service.

CONCLUSION

The Internet has become a tool that is accessible to and adopted by Americans in communities across the nation. Approximately two million more people become Internet users every month, and over half of the population is now online. Those who have been the least traditional users –people of lower income levels, lower education levels, or the elderly – are among the fastest adopters of this new technology. As a result, we are more and more becoming a nation online: a nation that can take advantage of the information resources provided by the Internet, as well as a nation developing the technical skills to compete in our global economy.

The expanding use of the Internet at schools, work, and libraries has played a significant role in this development. Young people are now active users of this technology. This report has demonstrated that the presence of computers and Internet access at schools is making these resources available to children who lack them at home. This means that our children will gain the skills and familiarity with new technologies that will allow them to find jobs in our new economy.

In addition, many more Americans than in years past are using computers and the Internet at work. Certain jobs that previously involved only manual labor, for example, now involve some use of information technologies. Proficiency with these technologies has become increasingly important, and adults are gaining such proficiency as more use information technologies at work and find new opportunities for using them at home.

Our nation has passed a significant milestone now that the majority of Americans use computers and the Internet for their daily activities. This trend is enriching our world, facilitating our work lives, and providing a skill set needed for a growing economy.

METHODOLOGY

This report utilizes data from the Department of Commerce's U.S. Census Bureau, taken from the Census Bureau's September 2001 Current Population Survey (CPS) of approximately 57,000 sample households. The survey took place during the week of September 16-22, 2001 and generated response rates of 93.5 percent for the basic CPS and 92.1 percent for the Internet and Computer Use Supplement.

The households surveyed were selected from the 1990 Decennial Census files with coverage in all fifty states and the District of Columbia. The sample is continually updated to account for new residential construction. The Census divided the United States into 2,007 geographic areas, each typically comprised of a county or several contiguous counties. A total of 754 geographic areas were selected for the 2001 CPS survey.

For each household, Census Bureau interviewers spoke to a person (called the "respondent") who was at least 15 years old and was considered knowledgeable about everyone in the household. For purposes of collecting data at the household level (such as type of connection to the Internet), the respondent provided information pertaining to the "householder" or "reference person," who is an adult in the household who either owns or has signed for the rent on the residence. For purposes of collecting data at an individual level, the respondent provided responses for him or herself and proxy responses for all other members of that household. The survey therefore provided information on 137,259 individuals (age 3 and older).

The Census Bureau cross-tabulated the information gathered from the CPS according to specific variables, such as income, race, education level, household type, and age as well as by geographic categories, such as rural, urban, and central city, plus state and region. The Census Bureau determined that some of the data were statistically insignificant for meaningful analysis because the sample from which they were derived was too small.

All statistics are subject to sampling error, as well as non-sampling error such as survey design flaws, respondent classification and reporting errors, data processing mistakes and undercoverage. The Census Bureau has taken steps to minimize errors in the form of quality control and edit procedures to reduce errors made by respondents, coders, and interviewers. Ratio estimation to independent age-race-sex-Hispanic population controls partially corrects for bias attributable to survey undercoverage. However, biases exist in the estimates when missed people have characteristics different from those of interviewed people in the same age-race-sex-Hispanic group.

Index

A

administrative support, 72-75
age distribution, 15, 83
age, 6, 7, 10, 14-17, 19-21, 26, 36-38, 49,
   53-55, 58, 63-66, 71, 76, 79, 82, 83, 86,
   89-92, 94, 96, 101, 111, 118
Asian American /Pacific Islanders, 24
Asian Americans, 49, 59

B

bank online, 38
Blacks, 24, 49, 92
broadband access, 45
broadband connections, 7
broadband, vii, 43-45, 54, 113, 116

C

cable modems, 1, 43
carpal tunnel syndrome, 88
cell phones, 7, 45-47
Census Bureau, 1-3, 7, 10, 12-14, 16-19,
   21-23, 25, 27, 36, 37, 39-41, 44, 45,
   48-51, 54-56, 57-66, 69, 72-80, 83-90,
   93-95, 117, 118
chat rooms, 38, 66

children, 7, 15, 17, 19, 53-56, 58, 59, 61-
   63, 65-67, 70, 82, 94-96, 98, 111, 117
college, 20, 54-56, 72, 73, 92, 95
communication, 47, 65, 66
community centers, 48
computers, vii, 1, 7-10, 46, 53, 54, 56, 58,
   59, 70, 71, 74, 78, 81, 82, 89, 111, 113,
   116, 117
confidentiality, 96, 97
Current Population Survey (CPS), 1-3, 7,
   10, 12-14, 16-19, 21-28, 31, 34, 36, 37,
   39-41, 44, 45, 48-51, 54-66, 69, 72-81,
   83-90, 93-95, 101, 104, 117

D

demographic groups, 94, 97
demographics, 7
Department of Commerce, 1-3, 6, 7, 10,
   12-14, 16-19, 21-23, 25, 27, 36, 37, 39-
   41, 44, 45, 48-51, 54-66, 69, 72-80, 83,
   84-90, 93-95, 97, 117
deployment, 44, 45
dial-up service, 43, 45, 116
dial-up, 43-45, 116
digital subscriber line (DSL), 1, 43, 45, 54
Digital Workplace, 71, 116
disabilities, 8, 81-85, 87-90
disabled, 86

E

e-commerce, 36
education, 6, 10, 20-22, 79, 89-92, 97,
    111, 113, 114, 116, 118
e-mail, iv, 26, 35, 36, 38, 40, 45, 65, 71,
    74-77, 88
employment status, 6, 85
English, 25, 26
entertainment, vii, 65, 66
entertainment-oriented activities, 38

F

family income, 11, 12, 21
farming, 73, 77
Federal Communications Commission
    (FCC), 43, 44
female Internet users, 37, 38
female-headed households, 60, 63, 67
fishing, 73, 75, 77
forestry, 73, 75, 77
friends, 97

G

gender, 6, 17, 72, 76, 96
Gini coefficient, 112-116
Gini efficient, 113
government services, vii, 36, 40
growing economy, 117
growth, 10, 13, 16, 17, 23, 24, 43-45, 76,
    77, 92, 111

H

health information, 38, 84
health services, 37, 40
hearing, 82-85, 87, 88
high school diploma, 20, 73
high school graduates, 92
higher income households, 13, 93
higher incomes, 21, 50, 93, 116
higher levels of education, 21, 111

high-income, 11, 45
Hispanic population, 25, 118
Hispanics, 24, 26, 27, 49, 92
households, 1, 6, 11-13, 17, 19, 21, 23, 26,
    40, 44-47, 53, 59-61, 63, 67, 78, 79,
    91-97, 101, 112, 113, 116, 117

I

income, 7, 10-13, 21, 22, 26, 36, 40, 45,
    49, 50, 58, 61, 63, 79, 89-91, 93, 97,
    111-116, 118
inequality, 8, 111-116
information technologies, 1, 2, 8, 53, 117
information technology, 77
instant messaging, 35
Internet subscriptions, 54, 67, 93, 94, 111,
    116
Internet traffic, 26
Internet usage, 104

J

job searching, 38

L

labor force, 13, 28, 31, 34, 86, 87, 101,
    104
language spoken, 26, 92, 101
libraries, 6, 48-50, 116, 117
list servs, 38
location of use, 48
Lorenz Curve, 112, 113, 115
lower family incomes, 26, 91
low-income, 11

M

male Internet users, 37, 38
male-headed households, 60, 63, 67
manual dexterity problems, 82
manual labor, 117
married couples, 19, 67, 94

mobility, 43, 82, 87
movies, 38, 45, 66

N

network effects, 97
news, 35-37, 39, 40, 65
non-Internet-using population, 92

O

occupations, 22, 72, 73, 77, 111, 116
online activities, 7, 35-37, 39, 40
online banking, 35, 36
online communications, 26
online purchases, 35, 39
online trading, 36
Organization for Economic Cooperation
    and Development (OECD), 5, 26

P

Pacific Islanders, 24, 49, 59
people with disabilities, 81, 82, 84, 90
personal digital assistant (PDA), 6, 46
play games, 65, 66, 84
playing games, 38, 66
product and service information, 35, 39
product/service purchases, 36
product/services, 36
public libraries, 49, 50, 64

R

race/ethnic category, 24
radio, 38, 45, 66
repetitive motion disorders, 88
retired, 86
rural areas, 44, 95
rural, 22, 23, 36, 44, 95, 118

S

school assignments, 37, 65
school, 1, 7, 20, 37, 47-50, 53-59, 61-63,
    65, 66, 70, 73, 79, 83, 91, 92, 95, 111,
    115, 116
schools, 1, 6, 56, 81, 117
search for information, 36
single-parent families, 59, 63, 94
Spanish, 26, 27, 92, 101
sports information, 35

T

teenagers, 15, 55, 65, 66
telemedicine, vii
television (TV), 38, 41, 45, 46, 66, 67, 97
trading online, 38

U

unemployed, 13, 31, 34, 86, 87, 94, 101,
    104
urban areas, 44
urban households, 23
urban, 22, 23, 36, 44, 118

W

weather, 35, 37, 40, 65
Whites, 24, 49, 59
women, 10, 17, 37, 38, 72, 73, 76
work, 1, 6, 7, 22, 48-50, 57, 65, 71-4, 76-
    79, 81, 88, 111, 115-117
workplace, 1, 8, 70, 71, 78, 79

Y

young adults, 7, 15, 53-56, 63, 65, 66